Ireland's Entrepreneurial Elite

Richard Curran and Declan Hayes

BLACKHALL
Publishing

This book was typeset by Gough Typesetting Services for
BLACKHALL PUBLISHING
26 Eustace Street
Dublin 2

e-mail: blackhall@tinet.ie

ISBN: 1 901657 35 3

A catalogue record for this book is
available from the British Library.

Printed in Ireland by
Betaprint Ltd.

To all those who strive for success

Contents

Foreword

Ten years ago this book would have been a mere pipe dream because many of those featured in this excellent collection of portraits had yet to achieve the status they now enjoy. Back then it looked as if the economy was destined to be reliant on the commitment by multi-national companies to set up in Ireland to create badly needed jobs. While foreign investment has been a vital contributor to our economic stature, the evolution over time of a vibrant crop of business people, confident in their ability to succeed in the cut and thrust of domestic and international commerce, has been a most welcome development in recent years. Irish business has begun to come of age.

It is not that long ago when businesses here caught in the transition to a post-industrial society required a State lending agency to keep them afloat. During that traumatic evolution the future appeared bleak even to those who wished to think otherwise. Debates raged about the absence of a business ethic. Profit, we were told, was a dirty word and that as a people we resented the success of others.

How could a business class emerge out of such a hostile environment was the subtext of much of what was being written and discussed for what seemed an interminable period of time. But lurking behind that smokescreen of sterile debate something dynamic was beginning to take root in the State. New business leaders – some without any tradition behind them – were beginning to make their mark on the economy.

Our entry into the EEC in 1973 was a step in the right direction. Investment on a scale we had never before witnessed started to flow from Brussels to all parts of the country. Major food groups took advantage of what Europe had to offer and overseas firms began to put down roots.

People began to sense that Ireland could indeed, work to profit from the changing economic world order. For some of us that transition was agonisingly slow and even the overseas sector disappointed from time-to-time. But as the seeds of the modern economy began to take root the perception that Ireland was destined to be the beggar of Europe began to change. Several factors, too many to detail in this short introduction, started to influence (for the better) how we saw ourselves within the broader European context.

Slowly but surely, Irish companies began to make an impact. The dialogue changed. Receiverships gave way to take-overs, as businesses here discovered they were more than capable of rubbing shoulders with the best. Now we have a small but growing bank of home grown multinational companies respected across the globe and Irish firms are beginning to make an impact that seemed highly unlikely a decade ago.

The success stories dealt with by Richard Curran and Declan Hayes in this series of profiles bears out the view that Ireland Inc has come of age. Gone forever is the self doubt that we could not hack it in the highly competitive world of modern business. One of the best yardsticks by which to gauge the state of health of any economy is the level of wealth it is generating. Over the past few years in particular the number of individuals who have joined the millionaire classes has begun to take off. This is good – creating wealth is what entrepreneurship is all about.

Given the current strength of the economy it is a fair assumption that in another few years the next undertaking of this kind will have to be at least twice as big to do justice to the thriving entrepreneurial class that will have emerged by then. Finally this book is a tribute, not just to those whose achievements are too often denied the recognition they deserve, but to the indefatigable spirit of a people who have brushed aside the obstacles that not so long ago, seemed insurmountable.

Dan Flinter
Chief Executive
Enterprise Ireland

July 1998

Introduction

> And he gave it for his opinion that whoever could make two ears of corn or two blades of grass to grow upon a spot of ground where only one grew before, would deserve better of mankind and do more essential service to his country, than the whole race of politicians put together.
>
> *Gulliver's Travels*, Jonathan Swift (1667-1745)

Just as in Swift's time, we still need entrepreneurs who can coax those two blades of grass to grow where only one previously grew. We also need people who can harvest and market those extra blades of grass. Most importantly, we need to give our grass-growing entrepreneurs their due and try to harness their energies and visions for our common good. This is our basic point, which we shall elaborate throughout this book.

In chapter one, by reviewing Ireland's recent performances, we shall suggest how current government expenditures could be better focused to aid our economy. In chapters two, three and four, by interviewing a variety of our most successful entrepreneurs such as – Carol Moffett, Eddie Haughey, David McKenna, Martin Naughton, Denis O'Brien and Ray Kearns – we point to where change can best be effected for our common good in both our industrial and services sectors. Chapter five deals at length with our food industry and, by interviewing Geoff Read, John Teeling, Denis Brosnan and a range of other practitioners from this, our most vital industry, shall point to how we can transform it to allow us to prosper as a nation in the future. Chapter six incorporates the views of our small business sector, our key policy-makers and our financiers. Chapter seven reviews the performances of those we interviewed in the months prior to publication and concludes with a series of recommendations based on their interviews and experiences.

Because these people have achieved so much in their respective endeavours, we believe that our policy-makers should, at the very least, address their concerns about the industries they know so well. Our policy-makers should also incorporate the views and energies of Ray Kearns and his educational empire into their exporting strategies. More importantly, they should foster a business culture where the successes of these people can be more easily replicated in the future.

This, then, is an optimistic book, pointing out what we, as a nation, can reasonably hope to achieve with the resources we possess and the market conditions we must collectively face. We show where our resources have been misapplied in the past and point to where they could be better applied in the future. We know that it is easier to propose than to dispose. That is why we finish with a short list of suggestions, which details where we believe that both debate and action should be focused in the years ahead.

As journalists and academics, we have done our professional duty by bringing these matters to the fore in a forthright manner. We point out that our entrepreneurs have, by Swift's dictum, done theirs. We hope that our politicians will eventually do theirs. We also hope that you, the reader, will do yours, by helping to expedite the necessary transformation of our society which we propose.

We thank our collaborators for doing their duty. In particular, we thank Forbairt and AIB for their logistical help and advice in bringing this project on-stream. We thank all of those people we interviewed. We thank our publishers and our colleagues, friends and families for their help and consideration. The usual caveats, of course, apply and all editorial view-points, mistakes, short-comings, oversights and the like are the responsibility of the authors alone.

CHAPTER ONE

Ireland in Brief

It would never be spring, always autumn
After a harvest always lost,
When Drake was winning seas for England
We sailed in the puddles of the past
Chasing the ghost of Brendan's mast.

from *Memory of Brother Michael*, by Patrick Kavanagh

Our national tendencies to begrudge and to look backwards to our non-existent golden age have only one redeeming characteristic: they are the perfect place to begin this book. That is because our cultural impediments remain the greatest single obstacle to achieving sustained economic growth in this island of ours. Until we stop living in the puddles of the past and denigrating the successes of those who are trying to build us a viable future, we will never succeed. Such has been our history, such will be our future unless we reform to allow our entrepreneurs the say they deserve in determining our future.

Ireland, alas, currently lacks a native entrepreneurial cadre of the requisite quality: Tony O'Reilly, Michael Smurfit, Eddie Haughey, Martin Naughton and their type are comparative rarities in Irish society. Begrudgery is, perhaps, a major reason for this national short-coming. Simply put, Ireland has been inimical to entrepreneurial culture. Our colonial, dependent past, with the consequently high demand for security in the form of permanent and pensionable jobs, our anti-business educational and social culture, have long bedeviled us. In a word, our begrudgery!

Although begrudgery is not the sole preserve of the Irish – Australians, for example, bemoan the success of their fellow countrymen – what is remarkable about Ireland is how entrepreneurs as diverse as Denis O'Brien and Tom Roche have highlighted and acknowledged its permanent, pernicious, invidious and insidious influence. They are not alone. Eddie Haughey, Denis Brosnan and David McKenna, amongst others, comment at length about it, as shall be seen in later chapters.

Our begrudgery has ensured that we have traditionally held our achievers in low esteem. Popular sentiment regards them as irredeemable rascals, rogues who would be more at home in a pack of rampaging Cossacks than at the helm of Irish business. The stark reality is, that because very few individuals have the proper mix of drive, inherent resources and sheer luck to be successful business-people we should, as a matter of national policy, nurture the very few that we do have. We wish to help abort these, our more negative cultural traits, and to thereby beget a more vibrant Ireland, where risk-takers are admired, aided, rewarded and respected. For this new Ireland to emerge, many things will have to change and change utterly. However, the cultural metamorphosis required is already occurring – this book shows how our entrepreneurs are presently transforming Irish business culture and, in the process, guaranteeing our collective future in the process. This process of change has been, and will continue to be, long and painful. The Monaghan of Patrick Kavanagh's youth, like the Dublin of his later years, is gone, never to return. More change, equally painful and poignant, is on the way. We must accept the reality of change and meet it head-on.

The demographic imperative to re-engineer probably overshadows all other forces. The combined trend of lower birth and mortality rates leads inexorably to an ageing population with fewer skilled workers to fund them. Dr Brian Aylward, chairman of the Irish Association of Pension Funds, has pointed out that Ireland's public pension bill will double to £2.4 billion in the next twenty-five years. Our skilled workers, who are now reaching retirement age, cannot be replaced from the ranks of the unskilled unemployed.

Currently, one in ten workers is unemployed; half of these have been unemployed for a year or more and it is highly likely that they will still be signing on in a year or more's time. Our small work-base cannot sustain the taxes these demographic imbalances demand. We cannot permanently accept the low living standards which these excessive taxes put on us, nor can class warfare or other divisive forms of social upheaval be an acceptable solution to our economic problems. Our only viable solution is to transform our society to make us more productive. We must abandon the dead-weight in our cultural baggage.

Begrudgery has not been our only cultural bug-bear. Our many social and economic failures can, ultimately, be traced back to the foundation of the State and the civil servants the British dumped on it as part of the leveraged buy-out which we call Irish Independence. The social and business conservatism of this imperial residue stifled both social mobility and social opportunity. They ensured that each of us found our own level within the Irish Free State's social caste system. At the top, our businesses became over-dependent on State-dispensed grants and, as a consequence, real native entrepreneurship failed to flourish. At the bottom, the less fortunate became dependent on dole hand-outs.

Independence, crucially, left unaltered Britain's imperial system of administration. An incredible ninety-eight per cent of the emerging Free State's civil servants had formerly been in the employ of the British administration. Neither their politics nor their work-rates changed. Low gear remained their preferred gear.

The consequences of this lethargy remain with us. Today, our civil service and related semi-State bodies account for a third of all employees, putting another ultimately unsustainable strain on the national exchequer. When we consider the vast amounts of tax-payers' money which has been pumped into resuscitating the corpses of Irish Steel, NET, CIE and similar semi-State bodies, the need for a fundamental reappraisal and re-engineering of our business culture becomes that bit plainer. For the Celtic Tiger to continue roaring, our entrepreneurs must be given the lee-way they need. Experiences, such as the Bord na Mona fiasco, whereby its CEO, Dr Eddie O'Connor, was pilloried on technicalities having won market share, must not be repeated. The rest of the public service must become as entrepreneurial as O'Connor made Bord na Mona.

We, the authors, are far from alone in criticising this mismanagement of our nation. ISME's Eoghan Hynes, albeit in somewhat cavalier fashion, dismisses our civil service leadership as the intellectual heirs of the Norman robber barons who bled us dry with their self-serving taxes in the 12th and 13th centuries. The role of the civil service in the Ireland of the future must, like its role in former days, be reassessed and then transformed if we are to become a viable economic entity.

The civil service is not our only excess baggage. As later chapters show, other entrepreneurs we interviewed also bemoan the oceans of money which have been squandered on Irish Steel, Team Aer Lingus and a host of other ailing semi-State endeavours. Although all of them understood the political imperatives which forced successive governments to yield to these sectional demands, none of them could adequately explain why our leaders remained so heavily engaged for so long in so many loss-making ventures in hotel and motel management, in transport, in turf and steel production, in arts and sports promotion and in television and telecommunications renting.

Sustainable development demands a radical reappraisal of our comparative advantages: both the traditional ones of fertile fields and the non-traditional ones of fertile minds which Glen Dimplex and others have harnessed. Job feather-bedding policies favoured certain lobby groups could provide some extra employment here – at a cost. It would, however, be a 'back to the future' solution, simply because we would not be moving with the technological times in which we live. Jobs, beyond their technological sell-by date, are not sustainable. Our entrepreneurs recognise this reality. Our politicians should follow their lead, kill off our semi-State dodos and put the resulting savings into building those industries and services where we can, in the future, retain a competitive edge.

We cannot have our cake and eat it. Either we continue to pay homage to the utopia of the tax-guzzling semi-State or we join the modern world. We can fund our semi-State white elephants by taxing our golden geese to extinction or we can face tomorrow with an alternative, more realistic strategy.

Our low skill-base must change if we are to face tomorrow's challenges with confidence. Our electronics industry, for example, is more heavily biased towards unskilled production work than is its counter-part in either Britain or the USA; its overall skill profile is, nonetheless, actually higher than the Irish average. We are not, in other words, necessarily the young, educated, sophisticated Europeans that our own propaganda tells us we are. We still have a lot of catching up to do. More importantly, we must recognise our short-comings and restructure accordingly. We must allow people like Ray Kearns, who set up Ireland's most successful private educational establishment, Denis O'Brien, who founded 98FM and whose Esat company has successfully challenged Telecom Eireann's monopoly, Eddie Haughey, who has made Norbrook Laboratories an international success, and all of our other talented entrepreneurs to play as full a part as possible in shaping our future. Either we revert to the failed policies of the past or we re-engineer for the future. There is no third path.

Our government must acknowledge this reality and act accordingly. They must coax Irish industry into building strategic alliances, usually as minority partners, with non-Irish concerns. Typically, many of these will be with our traditional trading partners, Britain in particular. These alliances will entail many changes in our traditional modes of thinking on such thorny issues as sovereignty.

Carol Moffett has called for the need to make our school-children more self-confident. The government must work to ensure that an entrepreneurial culture, based on self-sufficiency, replaces the selfish, parasitical outlook which is currently gaining so much ground here. Ireland has, for example, recently developed the unenviable reputation of being one of the world's top slip-and-sue country with outrageously high levels of liability litigation. The gigantic size of our court awards means that our entrepreneurs, especially those in the services sector, are forced to select lawyers rather than engineers or other more productive professionals as their closest advisers. Ireland cannot afford a standing army of a 100,000 over-dressed and over-paid lawyers! Stifling EU policies, which are making it a criminal offence for publicans to bar potential trouble-makers, seem hell-bent on ensuring that our litigation industry alone remains bullish. Ireland cannot sustain the closure of a 100,000 public houses!

These are no idle quips. The Medical Protection Society has studied actuarial reports on the trends in medical negligence claims in Ireland. As a result, they expect one in five Irish consultants to be sued over the next year. Both claim sizes and claim rates are significantly higher than are those of Britain and similar countries. Claim sizes are rising by ten per cent a year, claim rates by five per cent. Clearly, this is a growth industry which must be legislated away.

The high cost of public risk insurance ensures that entrepreneurs catering to the tourist industry and other people-focused sectors cannot guarantee themselves the future their endeavours entitle them to. Insurance companies are also damaged by the high premiums they must charge. We all suffer as a result. Many of us suffer directly by being sued. More suffer indirectly because our best companies are as aware as the rest of us of this new threat to their well-being. They observe our serried ranks of solicitors. When possible, they relocate. There have been several examples of this in recent years, including the Seagate closure in Clonmel.

Unemployment remains a most serious and seemingly intractable problem. Profound transformations are needed to re-integrate the long-term employed into the value-added process. Grant-aided industry, for example, currently takes less than twenty per cent of its workers from the live register. This is because the long-term unemployed do not have marketable skills. These and similar home-truths must be admitted if we are to re-orient ourselves to face the future with the necessary levels of confidence.

Before the Irish National Organisation for the Unemployed and similar organisations are allowed to join the national partners in determining government policy, they should organise themselves sufficiently to tell us what marketable skills they have. We, in turn, must recognise that the function of the private sector is not to provide employment for others. The business of business, is simply that: business. Our political culture must change to reflect this business reality. Consultation and consensus is all very well: economic growth and political leadership is even better. We must find ways of bringing the long-term unemployed into the work market with dignity. The key is training.

Our government must ease the path to success for our entrepreneurs. The costs and complexities of doing business in Ireland's fragile market act as barriers to our prospective entrepreneurs and other wealth-creators. Our policy-makers must, therefore, take the reality that Ireland is a second-rate place to do business in into account. We must change.

The IDA, for example, paints Ireland as a land of young, educated technocrats. The reality is strikingly different. General adult education levels are much lower than the OECD average. Educational standards pertaining in our agricultural sector are particularly low, with over half of the agricultural labour-force possessing no qualifications and less than twenty per cent having a Leaving Certificate or higher. This acts as an impediment on growth and is mirrored in the relatively low value-added component which agriculture gives our economy. The old refrain that if the Dutch ruled Ireland, they'd feed Europe and that if the Irish ruled Holland, we'd all drown still rings true: partly because our educational policies have ignored our major fixed asset: the fertile lands of Ireland.

Our deficiencies in qualifications and skills adversely affect productivity, competitiveness and, therefore, our overall prospects for sustained economic growth. We have not enough skilled, trained and talented workers to go around. Business cannot afford to slow down to train and hire over-priced apprentices. Stifling EU-inspired legislation makes them too expensive to hire – just as it has done in Holland.

With small firms, the most significant barrier to training is the absence of basic managerial skills which, in turn, perversely leads to a lack of awareness of the value of training. Lack of training in the past has resulted in a pool of Irish managers and supervisors who do not appreciate the importance of training for themselves or for their subordinates. A vicious circle of national under-performance sets in.

Our universities have a key role to play in redressing this dispiriting state of affairs and, indeed, Irish entrepreneurs and our more progressive educational institutions have attempted to resolve this mis-match between graduate supply and business demand. The Royal College of Surgeons, for example, in collaboration with UCD, have instituted an MBA to encourage the many entrepreneurs who have emerged from Ireland's medical ranks.

They are not alone. There is also activity further down the educational chain. The Irish Productivity Centre and nine Institutes of Technology have come together to offer a Business Planning Programme for owners and managers of small companies. UCC, through its wholly-owned subsidiary, Biotechnology (UCC) Ireland Ltd, provides facilities for the transfer of new technology arising from biotechnology research. It provides incubator units for food product companies in its Food Science Complex. It is also the base for the National Microelectronics Research Centre which is one of the best-equipped laboratories of its type in these islands. Similar examples abound.

Ireland also now has its own EU-funded innovation centres, modelled in part on the Strathclyde prototype. Each Business and Innovation Centre (BIC) is run by a small team of eight or nine people. Their relatively small size allows them to react swiftly to their client companies' needs and to make decisions quickly. Dublin BIC has a portfolio of some 152 companies, employing approximately 700 people in a variety of industries and services. The Dublin BIC introduced the concept of business angels to Ireland in 1989 and since then it has been pairing off private investors and new or young businesses seeking seed capital through a 'marriage bureau' operation. They have already raised over £500,000 in this way.

Some business-people feel there should be a one-stop shop where all their questions will be answered and all their needs fulfilled. This is unrealistic because all information is not contained in any one organisation. The learning curve is unavoidable: this is the first lesson they must learn.

In summary then, because a more educated, skilled and pliable workforce is needed, Irish education must be re-engineered so that it can add value to our economy. Other, less productive expenditures must also be trimmed back to saner levels. Social welfare largesse is the most obvious of these expenditures. The Irish Department of Social Welfare, which has proved quite entrepreneurial in marketing its skills to emerging nations, has an annual domestic budget of £4.5 billion. This colossal largesse, though going to the unemployed and other needy sections of the community, must be harnessed to maintain the momentum of economic growth. At the very least, it must be recognised that unless similar amounts are spent feeding the Celtic Tiger, recession and its consequences will inevitably follow.

A government, showing proper leadership, does much: subsidies, tax, education, health, regulations, anti-trust law, environmental laws, fiscal and monetary policy all help or hinder competition, these could –

and should – all be properly reformed to our common advantage.

Ireland cannot prosper if we squander the little wealth we have. We must husband our resources and harness them into more productive areas to guarantee our national well-being. If the private sector is to flourish, it must be given the necessary resources to do so. Irish society must therefore, be re-engineered – our government must downsize and then out-source its non-core activities, which should be defined in the narrowest possible terms; the clamber for pecuniary and compensatory rights must be balanced with communal responsibilities; those running for political office should set examples and voluntarily forfeit their rights to subsidised housing or to practice other costly, self-serving acts. Only those, like our entrepreneurs, who lead by example, should lead.

CHAPTER TWO

Industrial Ireland

Almost 250,000 people – a fifth of our total workforce – are directly employed in manufacturing. A further 200,000 non-manufacturing services jobs depend indirectly on this industrial base. The development of our manufacturing sector depends, in turn, on a variety of factors, including our government's policies on education, training, tax and income. Many of these policies are discussed elsewhere in this book – some others are outside of its ambit – however, the importance of all of these broader influences on industrial development highlights the need to ensure consistency across different areas of government policy.

Our industries have become much more high-tech over the last two decades and this trend, the rise of the high-tech sector at the expense of the others, is set to continue. High-tech industry is dominated by foreign companies which account for a whopping 96.5 per cent of net output and eighty-five per cent of employment in this sector. Productivity levels in these foreign-owned companies are high by international standards reflecting, among other things, the twin facts that they are concentrated in relatively fast-growing areas of high-tech industry and that they represent, in the main, the more successful elements of US and international industry.

Irish-owned industry, on the other hand, is very heavily concentrated in the low-tech sector there it accounts for over seventy-five per cent of both output and employment. Productivity levels amongst the Irish-owned firms are lamentably low by international standards, thus accentuating the gap in productivity levels between our high-tech and low-tech sectors.

Over ninety-eight per cent of the output of our high-tech sector is exported, compared with only about a third of the output of our indigenous industry. The geographical distribution of exports is also of concern. For paper and paper products, to take but one example, over ninety-six per cent of exports goes to one destination, Britain. The comparable figure for the high-tech sector is less than twenty per cent. Our loss of domestic markets, our generally low level of export performance and our over-reliance on Britain as an export target-market, all epitomise the relative weakness in competitive terms of substantial segments of Irish manufacturing industry.

More basically, the weakness of our indigenous industry points to our fundamental lack of competitiveness, reflecting deep-rooted structural deficiencies in respect of management, marketing, product development and innovation, as well as more immediate cost and finance-related constraints. Our industries, as they now stand, are too basic, almost primeval.

For much of Irish industry, competitiveness continues to be synonymous with basic cost-competitiveness. Given the very low levels of profitability obtained in Irish industrial firms, with the average return on sales amounting to a miserable 3.6 per cent, even fairly modest increases in costs can mean the difference between a profitable enterprise and a dodo. Moreover, given the heavy concentration of Irish industry in traditional sectors such as clothing and footwear or textiles, where payroll costs account for as much as a third of total sales revenue, it is clear that labour costs must rank as an important debilitating element of achieving an overall cost competitiveness.

While this cost competitiveness may be a necessary prerequisite for the survival of Irish industry, it is not a sufficient condition. The low level of profitability in Irish industry itself reflects a series of structural deficiencies, for which low costs can only partially compensate. These structural constraints need long-term re-engineering remedies.

We return to these topics when we discuss the food sector in greater detail in chapter five. For the moment, we explore three Irish firms, Moffett Engineering, Norbrook Laboratories and Glen Dimplex, all of which have achieved equally noteworthy successes in their respective, very competitive, fields.

CASE STUDY – MOFFETT ENGINEERING COMPANY LTD

The Monaghan-based Moffett Engineering Company is a good example of how Irish companies, when suitably re-engineered, can succeed in cracking new markets. Moffett also exemplifies the benefits of developing research and other linkages with our indigenous food industry. This has been evident in the development of its products, many of which were originally designed in conjunction with the Kerry Group and similar firms.

Moffett Engineering was established in the early 1940s by Cecil Moffett. It was a local engineering work-shop, principally engaged in designing, manufacturing and repairing agricultural machinery in Clontibret, County Monaghan. With the increased mechanisation in agriculture, the business developed steadily. New local industries such as mushroom farming, furniture manufacturing and poultry processing gave further opportunities to the company. They began to manufacture and sell machines such as clamps and presses which were designed especially for these industries. In the 1960s, Cecil Moffett saw a market gap in these emerging industries. They all needed a steel-cutting saw, which cost over £2,000 for a basic model. Cecil Moffett developed a steel-friction cutting saw called the 'monocut' saw which he could profitably sell for £300.

EU membership brought new challenges to the company. Building on increased EU funding and utilising the new dry-mix technology to manufacture fencing posts and slats, they targeted the farming sector and helped them to modernise. They immediately developed their own prototype for the production of dry pre-cast concrete products. Each individual machine was customised to the specifications of the individual customer. In the late 1970s, Moffett started to break into international markets. By the end of 1983, they were selling throughout the EU, Egypt, Sweden and Austria.

Because they were so highly dependent on the construction industry, sales were cyclical. They needed a machine with wide appeal that could be mass-produced and easily customised. They targeted Europe, where increasing wage costs and a growing mountain of legislation was increasing mechanisation. Moffett built on their skills in hydraulic systems. They designed a lift that could be mass produced but could also be customised and easily maintained.

EU legislation had stipulated that an individual employee could not lift more than 30kgs unaided. Moffett's Tail Lift was the first product to satisfy this criterion and Ireland's farmer co-operatives bought it. The main gain for Moffett in this enterprise was not pecuniary. It was exposure to transport operators. Kerry Co-op approached Moffett; the result was the 'Mounty'. Moffett worked closely with the Kerry Group, testing and improving the design of this new machine to ensure it could carry agricultural goods, without any difficulty, across wet fields. Initially designed for agricultural use, the Moffett Mounty has now six major areas of application: agricultural and horticultural supplies, poultry, construction, landscape, fire and rescue. Other miscellaneous uses, including waste materials handling, food, beverages, fuel and erecting marquees, have also emerged.

The Moffett Mounty is a rough terrain forklift that can be carried on the back of a truck. The all-wheel drive Mounty operates both as an all-terrain forklift and as a versatile loading/off-loading system in one tough package. The truck driver can single-handedly load the goods onto the truck at the depot, drive to the customer and place the goods exactly wherever they are wanted and because the Mounty easily traverses the roughest of terrains, it is ideal for deliveries to farmers and any other rough terrain residents. It is now the company's main product line, with annual sales exceeding 1,200 and markets in almost thirty countries. Demand is still bullish and, as a result, the company, one of Ireland's most successful, is still growing. Moffett has worked closely with core users in developing their products. The Moffett Mounty M2275, designed in conjunction with Monaghan Poultry Products, is now available in sixteen countries. The fact that the M2275 allowed Monaghan Poultry to lower their operating costs from twelve per cent to three per cent was not lost on other buyers world-wide.

It is still too early to assess overall market potential for the full range of Moffett's products. The market is in an early development phase and is, as yet, relatively small and immature. Carol Moffett believes that they could dominate the world rough terrain forklift market by the end of the century. With that objective in mind, they are concentrating on improving overall quality: their products, their marketing, their servicing and their market penetration.

Success, which is still not absolutely guaranteed, did not come overnight. As the Managing Director, Carol Moffett was aware that she had a very loyal workforce of 150 people and she was determined to ensure that their successes in the past would be continued into the future. To achieve these objectives, Moffett Engineering had, at great expense, to spend many years researching the needs of the distribution industry to convince them that the Mounty could revolutionise materials handling and distribution.

The immediate marketing task facing the company, once the prototype had been developed, was how to harness, in sales terms, the numerous applications the Moffett Mounty presented to the end user. They also wanted to penetrate Eastern Europe and further develop the US market. In addition, the company had to devote financial and management resources to their new product, the Moffett Multi Function Tractor. Both markets were considered essential to achieve the sales volume and market share required in order to underwrite the investments necessary to become the world's number one truck mounted forklift and to break into the tractor market. Though Princeton, Spyder and Brouwer arguably have slightly better and cheaper models than Moffett, Moffett's overall marketing and servicing approach makes them confident that they can achieve market dominance. At the moment they have just over twenty per cent of the growing world market in rough terrain forklifts.

The Moffett Mounty is manufactured in Ireland at their two factories in Clontibret and Dundalk. As well as providing much needed employment and other opportunities in those regions, Moffett's example shows that Irish entrepreneurs, when suitably focused, can succeed in international market niche areas.

Moffett's also shows how individuals and the companies they form can, despite the odds, succeed. Carol Moffett inherited the company at the age of nineteen when Cecil, her father died suddenly at the age of fifty-one. At the time, she was reading French and Spanish at Trinity College. She abandoned her studies and returned to Monaghan to confront the traumatic personal and professional consequences of her father's unexpected death.

Carol, in recalling both the challenges and the opportunities she faced says, "The business consisted of myself, a young nineteen-year-old woman, my brother Maurice, aged sixteen and two local loyal workers and a turnover of £20,000 per year. I built on my father's expertise. Although our customers sympathised with us on our bereavement, they wanted a service and I therefore had to know what I was talking about when I sought their custom. I set myself to learning the nuts and bolts of the business so that we could hold the customer base my father had developed. Hard work, dedication to our customers and to the needs of our banks got us over the worst days."

Moffett is very frank when she talks about how difficult it was to manage and build the business after her father's death. "I just felt that I had to do my best. There were too many things to do and a business there to run and I didn't hesitate in taking that on but it was tough."

Although she believes that most management skills can be taught, Moffett found that when she first began running the business most of these skills came naturally to her. "I discovered very early on that I had the ability to sell things to people. Nothing in business happens without sales. I found that if someone came in looking to buy welding rods I could also sell them a grinding disc. When it came to management, common sense prevailed and certain approaches just seemed logical to me. But I have to say at times it was just seat-of-the-pants tactics, which saw me through."

Carol developed a retail side to the business, selling the steel and bearings used in the production to the end users as well. That helped the company get over its initial cash flow problems. "My brothers, Robert and Maurice, later entered the business: Robert concentrated on design and Maurice took to the engineering side of the business. I now concentrate on international marketing, whereas Maurice keeps the domestic customers happy."

"I continue to work very hard and, though I like to get nine hours sleep a night, sometimes I have to work through till nine or ten at night. That's the price the small business person must pay."

Carol is aware that, in engineering, she is a woman in what is still very much a man's world. She recalls that although, when she took over the business at nineteen, some might have said she was a girl in a man's world, since then, all of her success can be attributed to "hard work, application, attention to customers and to all the necessary details of my business".

Although Carol Moffett believes that our national tendency to begrudge is still as pervasive as ever, she does not let it get her down. "I got where I am by hard work. That has given me confidence in my own abilities. Others can get the same confidence. Our educational system must be refocused to engender confidence into our kids: to make them believe in the very real entrepreneurial abilities that they do possess within themselves."

She also acknowledges that her company has succeeded in a sector in which Ireland does not have a strong industrial tradition. She attributes this success to a number of factors including the company's willingness to adapt its products for different customers. "We have always been dedicated to attending to customers' needs. If you succeed with a product in the British market, it will not necessarily be successful in Germany, because they will want certain changes. I try to explain to everyone in the company that our customers are our bosses because, at the end of the day, they give us the money to pay our bills."

Fast growth Irish firms, such as Moffett's, face a variety of other problems before reaching a stage where they can export to different markets and then tailor their products for each of these different markets. Research and development is vital for manufacturing businesses and because Moffett's traditionally supplied custom built machines, it always invested heavily in R&D, as Carol explains: "We have fifteen people working in R&D and we spend over five per cent of turnover on it. That is absolutely necessary in our business."

Proper bank finance is also essential if companies are to reach a stage where they can commit funds to R&D. "At this stage if we wanted finance we could go to the banks and get any amount of it. But smaller companies starting off need greater access to low cost finance. Financial people lose faith in the product easily. They often expect projected sales targets to be met too easily without factoring in the many vagaries of the market. The best laid plans of small firms, in particular, can often be blown off target by the responses of their competitors. Banks will have to be more flexible in allowing for the necessary vagaries of business."

Moffett Engineering currently employs over 250 people and has an annual turnover of over £30 million. While this amounts to well over 1,200 machines, only fifty of those will be sold in Ireland. At the time of interview, Carol stated her belief that her family would retain ownership of the company for some time to come, and she did not envisage selling it to a bigger market player. "I have always been impressed with the JCB company which is still privately owned by the same family. It has an annual turnover of £700 million. Once someone came up the lane and offered to buy the company on behalf of a client of his, but I think he had underestimated the size of Moffett Engineering and that was the end of that."

Carol Moffett believes many other Irish people can emulate her. "Let's face it. If a nineteen-year-old woman can bring a small business to where Moffett's is today, then anybody can do it. I threw all my talents and energies into the business. Others, who do the same, can only succeed as well."

CASE STUDY – EDDIE HAUGHEY'S NORBROOK LABORATORIES

Since it was started in 1969, Norbrook Laboratories, the veterinary pharmaceutical group, has been highly successful world-wide, employing nearly 1,600 people and generating an annual turnover of about £50 million in Europe alone. Senator Eddie Haughey, the millionaire Newry businessman, may have stepped down as managing director of the business he founded, but he believes that his new role as chairman will enable him to apply himself more to Norbrook strategy as well as to his other business and related interests.

The son of a County Louth farmer, Haughey emigrated to New York at the age of nineteen. He got his first job as an office boy in a pharmaceutical company, rising to become regional marketing manager after just six years. He was quick to realise that Europe would eventually follow the example of the US in setting rigorous standards for the pharmaceutical industry. He felt that if he were to use US standards as a basis for business back home, he would have a competitive advantage over his European rivals. Returning to Ireland in 1969, the year the Troubles began, he started to import pharmaceuticals from the Netherlands. He later went into production himself.

"The early days were, of course, hard. America had shown me the opportunities and the need to judge people on their bottom line. I returned to Ireland, knowing that I could compete in my chosen area of pharmaceuticals against the very best. The Italians, for example, were too narrowly focused to retain their market share over time. I saw the opening and I have worked hard ever since widening that initial opportunity."

"In the early days, the multi-nationals would rubbish my products to the vets. They had very strong marketing arms. I left the marketing to them and instead concentrated in sub-contracting in production for them. After I got a few production contracts from them, my credibility soared and more contracts followed."

So many contracts followed that Haughey's Norbrook Laboratories now control twenty per cent of the world market in the products they make. "We control over sixty per cent of the British market in veterinary products. We have eighty per cent of the Australian market, thirty per cent of the Canadian market and a small, but growing share of the American market."

Eddie Haughey has used the bottom line lessons he learned as a County Louth teenager in America to good effect. He still believes that companies should work by their bottom line, that they should make profits from the earliest possible time and that acquisitions and consequent downsizing should be made on that basis. To illustrate his point, Haughey recounts acquisitions he made in California. "I turned a US$20 million loss into a profit. OK, I had to fire 100 people to keep the other 200 jobs vibrant. That's the bottom line and my actions kept those 200 jobs vibrant. The alternative would have been the loss of all 300 jobs."

Today, Haughey owns ninety-five per cent of Norbrook and, aside from dividend payments, he is the highest paid executive in the North, earning £1.2 million a year. He is happy to work in the North and cites the traditional work ethic existing there as a factor in its favour. He sees his ability to use a UK brand as being enormously efficacious to him and cites the need for the South to develop a credible brand name.

Although he sees the group growing in the South – labour constraints, of course, allowing – he is adamant that any major acquisition he is likely to make in Europe would involve a manufacturing facility and that Ireland would therefore, not be his first choice of location.

As befitting a man running a global business empire, he is anything but provincial. However, he does recognise the advantages of operating from Ireland. He maintains that being based in Newry enabled him to hire graduates from both sides of the border. He has hired large numbers of technical and management graduates from Queen's and the University of Ulster. As he says: "Contrary to popular opinion, it is now becoming quite difficult to hire motivated workers who possess both useful skills and practical scientific experience. The problem is not so acute in the South but we have to grow where the skill base lies."

Although his eyes are firmly on keeping the bottom line in order, Haughey also believes in maintaining a happy corporate spirit amongst his employees. As part of that process, he has annual dinners, where all the staff and their families are invited. "Motivation and team spirit are essential to achieve on-going results. Although I act globally, I must also make sure that things in Newry and at my other plants are as they should be."

Haughey is often presented as leading something of an extravagant lifestyle. And it is clear that, while he enjoys the trappings of his wealth, he insists that each of the houses, three aircraft and antiques he owns, has its own specific purpose. Describing himself as an acquisitive man by nature, Haughey maintains that he enjoys things of beauty. He points out that each of his acquisitions furthers his business. The converted castle where he lives, on 400 acres in Rostrevor, County Down, is also Norbrook's farm research centre where extensive testing is carried out on animals in developing new veterinary products. The company has set up a number of joint ventures with other pharmaceutical firms and the farm has a permanent stock of 600 cattle, several hundred pigs and other targeted species. He also owns a house in Dublin's Fitzwilliam Square which he uses for his work in the Irish Senate, as well as a strategically placed house near London's Heathrow Airport.

"You must grasp both the overall picture as well as all the details to achieve success. Both my professional and private lives depend on a sound logistical base. I spend fifty per cent of my time travelling and selling, which are the vital cogs in the whole process I am involved in. I must travel, entertain and sell for days, sometimes weeks, on end. If I don't have my houses, planes, personnel and other logistical back-ups in proper order, I will pay a hefty price for that sloppiness. Although business must come before pleasure, they should go hand-in-hand. And that can only happen with proper organisation." For Haughey, starting up Norbrook and developing it to its present pre-eminent position required a lot of hard work and tough decisions, which have contributed to his image of being a shrewd business operator. And, with interests varying from aviation, shooting, fishing, researching the history of architecture and developing patents, Haughey holds strong views on a number of issues, including entrepreneurship itself.

While many things have changed in Ireland since Norbrook was established, other things, he maintains, have been slower to change. The begrudgery attitude to entrepreneurs is as strong as ever in Ireland, Haughey believes. Until entrepreneurs are held in the same esteem as solicitors, accountants and similar professionals, Ireland's entrepreneurial culture will not be transformed. "I wriggled into a market niche here in 1969. I have developed that niche into a sizeable international operation. Many Irish men and women have benefited from that niche. Surely, that deserves recognition and support."

Although Haughey divides the world into thinkers and doers, he believes that entrepreneurs, like himself, have the uncanny ability to marshall both of these attributes and produce something out of the resulting fusion. "If their ideas are original and applicable, then they will become successful entrepreneurs." He laments that Ireland has failed to give sufficient respect to business people who have created wealth from nothing. "I fix a deal each day. I buy or sell something every day. We must get more Irish people buying and selling. Although it looks easy, it is not." He also believes that we must begin to respect entrepreneurs, including those who try but fail. "In Ireland, if a business fails, our begrudgers run down and rubbish the failed entrepreneur. In the United States that same person's experience would be valued and built upon."

Although one of the successful number of border millionaires who have come to prominence in recent years, Haughey believes that we must plan our marketing approach on an island-wide scale to have any hope of achieving the desired economies of scale which are prerequisites for being a player in today's business world.

He is well aware of the advantages of operating from Newry. "Operating here in the early days allowed us to use a UK label and that was vital in gaining market share in Britain. People are, thanks to the standards of education pertaining here, well trained. They also have an industrial history and therefore tend to be well motivated."

However, because he believes that Ireland would make more sense as one economic unit, he disagrees with the recent special-status focus on border counties, which he dismisses as being short sighted. "Jobs in Mayo and Kerry are just as important as jobs in South Armagh or Louth. Ask anyone in Kerry. The ultimate goal should be an all-Ireland body for development, within which there is competition from different areas. One obstacle to this is the lower corporate tax rate in the South, but this problem could be bypassed by allowing for higher grants in the North. North and South, we must synchronise our activities to get the maximum kick for our buck."

On the subject of cross border co-operation, Haughey laments the fact that IDA Ireland in the South and the Northern Industrial Development Board are forced to compete instead of to co-operate with each other. "If Ireland was marketed on an all-Ireland basis, with higher grants in the North, start-ups needing cash could look North while continuing or expanding businesses could look at Southern locations."

Seven years ago, when Norbrook's annual European turnover was about £30 million, floating the company was considered but Norbrook later proved able to raise the necessary finances for expansion themselves. Flotation is still not ruled out as an option should future circumstances demand it. "A few years ago I did consider floating the business, but now I find that I can get the business to grow without doing that. Why do companies seek a listing in the first place? It is an important means of raising finance, but I now find I can raise the finance I need without the inconvenience of floating. Clearly though, we must make it easier to raise venture and equity capital here, if we, as a nation, are to grow."

Haughey points out that changes in the pharmaceutical sector are requiring companies to increase their expenditure on R&D in order to compete. Continually refined EU and FDA regulations also add to the expense. In the last five years, over 1,000 products have disappeared from the British market as the industry becomes more competitive. In this kind of competitive environment, Norbrook have to think globally and acquire more companies so that they can remain a global player in a global game.

He views his current European acquisition in this light. Within Ireland, the group already has major expansion plans. Norbrook currently has three factories in Newry, one in Monaghan, as well as one in Britain and another in Nairobi. Plans to expand these plants are well in train, as are plans to open another plant in Birr, County Offaly.

Haughey's belief system can be summed up in his focus on the bottom line. "I started this company with £1,200 I brought back from the States. I worked hard, suffered the usual problems of cash flow and pressure from the banks to pay off loans. I stuck at it and I succeeded by one golden rule: I never made a promise to deliver what I could not deliver. Hard work, hard selling, hard slogging did the rest. It is the same now as it was when I returned here in 1969."

Can Ireland sustain a big player like Eddie Haughey or will he leave Ireland if business demands it at some later stage? These are questions our leaders must ask themselves. We have incorporated the views of Eddie Haughey and other entrepreneurs into our book. Let us hope our legislators will do likewise when they decide business policy in the crucial years ahead.

CASE STUDY – MARTIN NAUGHTON'S GLEN DIMPLEX

Since Glen Electric began operations in Newry in January 1974, it has consistently exceeded all its growth projections. It was a most unlikely success story. It began as a green-field project in a neighbourhood with a bad political and commercial climate. The project was heavily dependent on State assistance, its initial workforce was unskilled and had a long and corrosive history of high unemployment behind them. Closures and bankruptcies were all too common in Newry at the time.

Newry was the scene of Seenozip, a company which is still, after almost forty years, quoted as the classical case of incentive abuse. In more recent times, Newry saw many closures, most of them as a result of the IRA's bombing and kidnapping campaigns. When Glen Electric began, Newry had already grown weary of politically expedient quick fix solutions to its interminable unemployment problems.

Martin Naughton believed he could succeed in those unpromising circumstances. Naughton was not born into wealth. The son of a Dundalk-based Garda, Martin Naughton emigrated to Britain and signed on as an engineer with a cruise liner after he finished his apprenticeship in the late 1950s. Before the cruise began, he met an old friend who persuaded him to return to work in Ireland where he eventually became works manager with AET in Dunleer. AET were then our main manufacturer of electrical goods. When EU entry made AET uncompetitive, Naughton sunk his modest life savings into forming a new company, Glen Electric.

Naughton is well aware of the begrudgery factor. "Setting up your own business gives a great sense of achievement. But there can be a big price to pay. There is a strain on family life. You risk your money, your home, your security and peace of mind. Worse still, you risk ridicule from our standing army of begrudgers. They are still with us."

After becoming managing director of the new company, at least two of his former colleagues joined him and the five original investors raised £50,000 between them. The bank arranged a loan for a further £20,000. The Northern Ireland Finance Corporation, having offered pound-for-pound backing, did slightly better with £80,000 which was half loan and half equity. Glen Electric, with £150,000 but with neither product nor track record, was born.

He initially concentrated on producing a simple range of heaters. Aiming for low cost production through high volume and low overheads, Glen spent its first three years consolidating and growing. By the fourth year, sales were, at £2 million, considerably above target and were still rising. Glen's marketing approach was simple but effective. It offered goods with the right matrix of price, quality and delivery time to suit the big British multiples, who placed more and more orders with Glen as its reputation spread.

In Britain, the Dimplex company, having poured much of its resources into the production of electric storage heaters when off peak electricity was being withdrawn from the tariffs, found itself in the hands of a receiver when oil prices soared in the mid-1970s. When the opportunity arose, Glen took over Dimplex. Naughton's £2 million bid for a generous proportion of Dimplex's assets was accepted and Dimplex became part of the growing Glen Electric empire.

Twenty five years ago, Glen Electric was a small electrical appliance manufacturer; now it employs 6,000 people world-wide, it has a £350 million turnover with a strong market presence in the US, Britain and other key markets. While just three per cent of sales are in Ireland, twenty per cent of its employment is based here. Glen Dimplex has, in other words, been of immense benefit to Ireland.

Although it is a conservative company, an audacious acquisition strategy has played a key role in Glen Dimplex's rise to prominence. As stated, in 1977, the then Glen Electric took over Dimplex, a company eight times its size; Morphy Richards, Burco Maxol, Westcan, Chromalox and Hamilton Beach have been among the many brand-name companies they have acquired since then.

Naughton remains delighted with the take-over of KKW, the highly profitable electric heating division of Siemens. "KKW was a very profitable acquisition. It was a great buy. We turned a good performer into a star performer and it has opened up many other doors for us. We now provide Siemens with all its heating products throughout Europe." More strategically, Naughton maintains that the KKW take-over allowed them to do business in Germany. "Germany is a key market and, unless you have a German brand-name, then you can forget about doing business there. KKW gave us the respected name we needed to conquer Germany." Elaborating on this point, Naughton maintains that a presence in the German market facilitates entry into the emerging markets of Eastern Europe. "The heaters, kettles, electric irons and other household appliances that we make are perfect for Poland, Hungary and those other countries beginning their ascent up the consumption curve."

Although massively successful, Glen's power reins are tightly held. Martin Naughton owns seventy-five per cent of the company. Lochlann Quinn, the elder brother of Labour Party leader Ruairi Quinn, owns the remaining twenty-five per cent. The company structure involves two holding companies. Because one of these is registered in Dublin and the other in Belfast, the company's financing strategy allows them to exploit tax disparities between the North and the South. Overall, however, because the company is debt free, the company is highly profitable.

Just how profitable it is, Martin Naughton is not prepared to say. In fact, because Glen Dimplex is an unlimited company, Naughton prefers to keep sensitive financial information on his company largely confidential. "We have been profitable every year since we commenced business. We have had no need to go public so far. We would only go public if an acquisition came along of a sufficient size that was strategically important to us that meant we had to go for resources. Alternatively, we might look at going public to position the company correctly for the next generation. However, we are still young and so that is not an immediate consideration."

Even though it is now a small multi-national in its own right, it is also a major employer in County Louth. Its two Dunleer plants employ about 800 people who service mostly the British market. And although he operates the company from Dunleer, Naughton maintains that the company is not a one-person operation. "Profit and attention to the bottom line are the key features of this company. Because we have such a good group of performers running our operations, when we took over Belling, we were able to put in our own team to run it."

Naughton wants his company to be even more successful and – even though he must contend with the competitive problems our EMU membership will inevitably bring – he has, for that reason, expanded the air conditioning systems section of the business. "Because we are so concentrated in heating, our business peaks in winter. So, air conditioning is counter cyclical for us. It will help our sales and productivity figures plateau out over the whole year. Europe is a £2 billion air conditioning market and if we can get two per cent of that market, we'd be very happy." He believes that we could become a components supplier to the centres of industrial excellence which are developing in Europe. "Italy, for example, has over 100 companies making electrical appliances. That will soon dwindle to single digit figures. They will have huge components requirements. That is where Ireland can come in."

Although now a successful international player who can speak from the rare perspective of an Irish entrepreneur who has truly developed a multi-national from scratch, Martin Naughton has not forgotten his roots. Nor has he forgotten how hard it was to get the original finance to set up Glen Electric. "The company can now borrow any amount it needs. There is no great problem at that end. There are, however, still big problems for those trying to borrow their initial start-up capital. It is something which must be addressed."

However, he believes that staying competitive is the key which opens up all the doors to success, and to the finances which are necessary to fuel that success. "If you are cost competitive, people will beat a path to your door. That at least has been my experience. The Programme for National Recovery has helped to give us the recent boom we are enjoying. Ireland is now more cost competitive than it was. That has to be good for everyone."

He favours further reform to make us competitive. "Take telephone charges. When it costs double to call Yorkshire from Dunleer than it does to call Dunleer from Yorkshire, that cannot help Dunleer. When you factor in our tax system, which makes it £10,000 more expensive to give a middle manager the same rate here as that which applies in Yorkshire, many businesses may begin to wonder whether they would be better off to operate from Yorkshire. The Government should ponder on these cost related realities of doing business here."

However, Naughton also points to the advantages of using Ireland as a base for building a multi-national conglomerate. "There's been a lot of hard work involved in building up the group. But, at the end of the day, it's about giving the customer what they want. It's as simple and difficult as that."

CHAPTER THREE

The High-Tech Sector

Moffett Engineering Ltd, Glen Dimplex and Norbrook Laboratories are not our only non-traditional successes. We shall now examine our hardware and software sectors, our current exposure to the Internet and finish with case studies from the telecommunications and entertainment sectors to show that Ireland can compete even in these most advanced fields. We conclude that, although there are risks aplenty in these areas, the rewards that properly focused and properly financed policies can beget are commensurately greater than they are elsewhere.

From a negligible base only twelve years ago, software has become our second largest export industry and may become our largest in the next few years. Yet of these exports many have come from twenty or so US multi-nationals. But indigenous software companies have already shown the world what they can achieve, for example the multi-million dollar flotations of Iona Technologies and CBT. A string of other software companies are expected to come to the market in the next few years. There are still possibilities for Irish software companies who position themselves well. Iona Software is one such company which began by acting as an agent for some of the smaller but more progressive USA-based companies.

Tim Daly, managing director of Iona, had experience in making other US companies successful in Europe and Asia, so he formed a republishing company to take the products of these minnows into the international market. The company focused on the home multimedia PC. Iona's model was based on taking proven products onto the international market place. Innovation was ignored as a consequence.

Numerous obstacles remained. First, when approaching financial institutions in Dublin, Daly found that they didn't understand the software business and, being reluctant to admit their ignorance, failed to ask the appropriate questions. These Irish-based venture companies also worried about Iona's lack of tangible assets, a common-place factor in the information industry where people and not machines are a company's critical assets.

Initial financing came from personal funds and from two external investors, one American and one Irish. Once the company had secured an outside investor, the IDA lent critical help. However, frustrated with the lack of progress in Dublin, Daly went to London to raise venture capital. The reception in Britain was much more positive than that he had experienced in Dublin. The company targeted the eight major British-based venture capital companies, four of which responded positively and two of which cancelled all their appointments to visit them in Ireland the following day.

The experience brought out a number of important lessons. The management realised the massive expenditure in terms of time and energy which raising money involves – about fifteen months in Iona's case – and the high percentage of management time it takes up – about fifty per cent in the early stages. The experience also gives important insights into the workings and rationale behind banks' thinking. One person in Dublin, on whom the company is still awaiting a call after many years, did give them some advice: most start-ups cost twice what the founders think and takes twice as long to get there but most importantly the business grows to twice what they originally thought.

Iona is not our only success story. CBT, the Irish-inspired, US-based computer-training group, has proved to be an outstanding share price performer. CBT is one of the great successes of the last few years. Founded in 1984, the company's fortunes soared when Bill McCabe engineered a management buy out in 1991. McCabe crucially forged strategic alliances with some of the big American software houses. He also switched the focus of the company to the American West Coast. CBT was floated on Nasdaq in early 1995. Since then, its share price has continued to sparkle. Many of the benefits CBT could have given the Irish stock market have been lost to the US market.

Although the issue of fast growth firms is central to our future prospects, companies like Iona, CBT and our other high profile IT successes can blind us to the other benefits we can reap from this area. The Internet, for example, has provided us with many unorthodox business success stories. Niamh Crowe, a freelance writer and founder of Speechwriters, a company providing speeches for weddings, banquets, anniversaries and other special occasions, is one such success story. Crowe's website has already attracted customers from Boston and Korea. The Cork-based Bizzee Bee company has also done well from the information superhighway, selling embroidery designs over the Internet. The company attracted three regular customers from the US through its website and continues to attract overseas enquiries.

There are many other positive developments as well. Online cafes have sprouted up in the unlikeliest of places. Kilnaleck in rural County Cavan boasts a cybercafe where punters can sip coffee whilst surfing the Net. Courses in information technology are being run for the locals, adults and children alike. The Kilnaleck community has also compiled an e-mail directory of Cavan people throughout the world and they send a regular county newsletter to those on the list. They intend sending football matches and other local events to Philip Sheridan's South Bend bar in New York's Bronx via Internet Phone or Real Audio.

Kenny's Bookshop in Galway is another interesting enterprise, which has successfully re-structured itself to avail of the opportunities which the Internet presents. Kenny's is a family run bookshop which specialises in Irish interest stories. It also operates two art galleries. Kenny's has generated new sales and increased profits by availing of this technology. Since the 1980s, the company has exported products to US libraries; in 1988 it appointed a marketing director to explore opportunities in the US market. Out of this grew the idea of establishing a presence on the Internet, the global network of thirty million computer users throughout the world. Kenny's Bookshop is now one of the major success stories of virtual reality Ireland. The Internet allows Kenny's to access 400 clients world-wide for the cost of a local call. The company's comprehensive site is based on the World Wide Web, which allows for graphics and images to be viewed and down loaded. Several sections are featured, including information on Irish authors and artists, a comprehensive catalogue of stock and a search and order facility.

Anyone can access the website and be taken on a visual tour of the shop, which includes accessing a list of all of the titles in stock. Des Kenny, who runs the business with his brother Tom, believes they were lucky with the Internet idea because they were initially approached by Ireland Online to take it up as a pilot project. Kenny, who completed a Master's Degree in Comparative Literature at the Sorbonne during the heady days of 1968, admits to being computer illiterate. "I always tried to hold the things at arm's length. But Ireland Online were aware of our mail order business and they approached us to give it a try. But it has worked extremely well in generating business."

In their pre-virtual reality days, a two to three month lead time, before new product information appeared in the company's printed catalogue, was the norm. Now that the catalogue appears in an electronic format, it can be updated twice a week.

Kenny's use of the Internet as a marketing and sales tool has also had a substantial impact on the company's profits. Des Kenny estimates that the network has contributed US$50,000 of repeat business from international clients. "We have book clubs with clients in forty different countries and all of the fifty states of the US. With the book club, twenty-five per cent to fifty per cent of new business has come directly from the Internet."

In Kenny's view, it would be quite easy for firms in similar businesses to use the Internet successfully, provided they had an unusual or niche market and provided they could adapt the Net to their specific product range. "It would be difficult to sell loaves of bread on the Internet but I have heard of one company selling turf on it. We are fortunate in that the nature of our business is selling culture and there is a massive market out there for Irish culture. We had to get out there and find customers internationally. If you think you can sit on your backside and wait for them to come in the door, then you can forget it."

These examples, though small in themselves, do show that we can profitably enter the modern, digitised world. Our next case study show that we can compete at the cutting edge as well.

CASE STUDY – DENIS O'BRIEN, ESAT & 98FM

After studying Arts in university, Denis O'Brien was appointed Tony Ryan's personal assistant for both GPA and Ryanair. Since then, O'Brien has built up his own mini-empire, which includes 98FM, and several other radio stations on the continent, a telecommunications company, Esat, which has not only embarrassed Telecom Eireann by poaching some of its big corporate clients, but even managed to secure the contract to provide telephone services to accountancy firm, Stokes Kennedy Crowley, at a time when its managing partner was chairperson of Telecom Eireann. Esat currently provides long distance services for thousands of companies, in a market which had been dominated by the State giant Telecom Eireann for years. Included amongst these customers are over twenty per cent of the Business and Finance Top 1,000 companies.

O'Brien's success story is not only interesting in itself; because it can, in part, be replicated, it is of wide practical relevance. He entered business for classical entrepreneurial reasons: to try to build up businesses in areas where he saw an opportunity. After his GPA experience, O'Brien linked up with Fred O'Donovan, the former RTE chairperson, and together they set up a company called Esat Television. Immediately, they sold off fifty per cent of Esat Television for £150,000 to six private investors. To finance his share, O'Brien initially worked three weeks of every month in the US in a family business selling horse products to retail outlets and setting up regional distributors. "This was real sales experience. I would arrive in Kennedy airport in the back of a plane having bought the cheapest possible ticket. I would hire the smallest American car I could find for $30 a day from a backstreet car hire company, plonk my box of samples in the boot, take the map and contact the local distributor's salesperson."

It was during these trips that O'Brien first saw the Home Shopping Network (HSN). This was a television business programme which specialised in retailing thousands of different products to approximately thirty-five million homes throughout the US. Convinced that his idea of setting up a shopping channel for Britain and Ireland was viable, O'Brien founded a mail order company called Grattan Next, to supply the product and take the orders. He contacted Rupert Murdoch's Sky Television, who made six hours of air-time available. "In the beginning, I had the money and he had the experience. In the end, he had my money and I had the experience. However, when we commenced operations, we had only 35,000 potential viewers in Britain. In the first month of operations we sold £14,000 worth of goods and lost £500,000. Clearly, we were in deep waters."

After pruning staff numbers, O'Brien hired an American 'ass kicker' who quickly turned the six hours of daily programming into a successful, American-style razzmatazz show. "We started to have a higher hit-rate of sales per potential viewer than even the US, but unfortunately, the damage had been done. We never got sufficient access to our customers."

O'Brien says the experience of failure was traumatic. Despite this failure, it is interesting to note that O'Brien had sufficient depth of character to bounce back. He obtained an FM licence for Dublin, and what has now become the flagship of Communicorp Group, 98FM, was born. "I didn't make the mistake of importing staffing practices or programme management from Montrose, choosing instead Aussies and Kiwis who had operated in deregulated home markets against cut throat competition for ten years. We researched listenership trends for seven months and identified the gap in the market. We established a colleague friendly, go-getting culture in cramped offices with second hand furniture. Then, we went for broke."

The station quickly reached and consolidated a twenty-five per cent market share and is now established as an attractive medium for advertisers. O'Brien bought fifty per cent of the radio station and, in its second year of operation, it made a £300,000 profit. It currently makes profits of about £1 million with no remaining bank debt.

In 1990 O'Brien turned his sights on Eastern Europe and, after a year of research and after securing £400,000 from private investors, he initiated Kiss 98FM in Prague. A year later, he entered the telecommunications market. Lethargy, alas, almost scuppered the plan. "For three years we dealt with a slob in the Department of Communications, whom we nicknamed 'Mount Etna', who had no understanding of and even less interest in the EU telecommunications Directives." These delays all but forced O'Brien's Esat company into liquidation. He had a second mortgage on his house and owed the banks about £500,000. In

1993, he went to see Fianna Fáil TD Brian Cowen, whom he had never previously met, and explained to him that Esat had a right to provide long distance services under EU Directives. Cowen quickly checked the facts and, in the face of sustained opposition from Telecom and sustained inertia from 'Mount Etna' and his colleagues, moved to award Esat a licence.

By the summer of 1994, the business needed at least £5 million in new investment which was more than could be generated internally. O'Brien pooled his radio and telecommunications assets into a new company and sold off a third stake to Advent International for an initial sum of US$10 million.

O'Brien's colourful experiences exemplify the sad fact that, in Ireland, it is easier to raise a large amount of money than it is to raise a small sum. This is because, apart from the Smurfit job creation fund, until relatively recently there had been virtually no source of venture capital available on realistic terms to small businesses. As O'Brien says: "It can be virtually impossible to raise £100,000 but financiers take you seriously when you want to raise £20 million. They must encourage more young people to borrow £100,000 in the hope that they will grow to be able to need to borrow larger sums."

He maintains that educational reform has the single most important role to play in re-engineering our business culture. "Traditionally, every Irish mammy dreams that her little darlings will grow up to be accountants, solicitors, priests, doctors: anything but a person who seeks to make a profit and create wealth – and therefore employment. We now also have a new sub-phenomenon of young people who come out of third level institutions with a confident bounce in their step and when asked what they would like to do, they reply: PR or marketing. In other words, anything but going in to land a sale!"

"People in Ireland will throw rocks and worse at you if you try to achieve something." Like other entrepreneurs to whom we spoke, he remarks how people look askance at successful business people and can believe only bad of them. O'Brien passionately believes that we must stop begrudging those who have earned their wealth from taking risks. "This includes recognising the real value to society of the successful enterprise, be it large or small. Our begrudgery ensures that entrepreneurial failure is frowned upon and mocked whereas, in the USA, the experience which failure engenders is highly prized. Above all, we should remove the stigma attached to efforts to develop a business that fails. The most important set of lessons which I have learned came, as I said, not out of books or case studies, but from seeing my business collapse and being responsible and accepting responsibility for it."

Although he holds forthright views on many subjects, O'Brien's ire is strongest when he discusses the State monopolies. "Even when the EU moves to deregulate, we often shoot ourselves in the foot by whinging for a derogation, which merely postpones at greater cost essential market adjustments. If Irish entrepreneurs are ready to enter major utility markets on a commercial basis, why can they not be free to do so?"

O'Brien points out that a lack of venture capital was a key obstacle to creating an entrepreneurial Irish base and that all of the main venture capital funds operating here are overly risk averse. He highlights the fact that these funds have invested in the Fitzpatrick Hotel Group and Heiton Holdings, the quoted hardware group and remarks that "while these are solid blue chip investments, they do not exactly characterise the supposedly risk-taking, path-breaking spirit we expect from venture capitalists". O'Brien believes that our leasing companies, which rent office furniture to our start-ups, are the closest thing we have to venture capital; he would like to see these companies expand to provide ancillary services.

Raising money is, according to O'Brien, a key problem our entrepreneurs must face. Because the necessary capital was not available here, they were forced to search offshore, usually in Britain, for it. Because of the more bearish attitude British investors tend to adopt to Irish projects, further time-wasting problems can emerge. "While Irish start-ups may have some success there, I believe that British-based financiers still have a negative impression of most facets of Irish business and this can be a problem. So Irish entrepreneurs resorted to their own private sources: their extended family, and friends to raise money, and that is where so much of the venture capital in this country actually comes from. Although it is good to see this money come into the process of wealth creation in Ireland, it is not enough. The proper facilities and channels must be there to allow our smaller entrepreneurs tap into corporate funds at attractive rates."

Further, although it is not the job of our high street banks to be venture capitalists, O'Brien criticises them for the way they structure and implement their charges. Similarly, he believes they are too conservative in so far as they still insist on an inordinate amount of personal guarantees. "Irish banks don't look at cash flow. In the US, banks always look at EBIT – earnings before interest and tax. Taking a less conservative approach would help here. Similarly, if the government and the pension funds were prepared to co-operate more in making low-priced funding available to our entrepreneurs, I think that would also be helpful."

O'Brien also criticises our over reliance on foreign companies and the inequities their preferential treatment gives rise to. "Imagine a foreign company coming to Ireland and setting up in Limerick and employing fifty people there. They pay ten per cent tax. I employ over 200 people in this country, and I pay a lot more. What makes the foreigner's jobs better than the jobs I have created? I think more people are starting to ask these kinds of questions."

More people are entering politics as career-minded professional politicians than ever before, and that this is having a detrimental effect on the quality of policies being developed. "We now have less business people going into politics than was the case in the 1960s and 1970s, when there were many more self-made entrepreneurs in politics. A lot of our current political leaders have never been in business. That must colour their judgement."

Business organisations are another bone of contention with O'Brien, who maintains we have too many self serving 'old boys' clubs'. He, somewhat controversially, sees the Irish Business and Employers Confederation (IBEC) as a 'colossus' which is heavily dominated by the semi-State sector. "It is a mouthpiece for monopolists. Modern day managers don't bother with IBEC, or another old boys' club, the Irish Management Institute (IMI). ISME lights the candle for the rest of us. I think organisations like the IMI need to be reformed."

Although O'Brien has plans to continue expanding his mini radio empire, opportunities in telecommunications are currently absorbing most of his efforts. Having been part of the consortium which won the second mobile phone licence, Esat has plans to expand rapidly. The licence fee was £15 million, but industry professionals now value Esat Digifone at about £100 million. The recent successful flotation of Esat also opens new opportunities, as the company develops its new telecommunications infrastructure in a joint venture with CIE.

Esat's big competitor is Telecom Eireann, against which O'Brien makes some stinging criticisms. "Telecommunications in Ireland cannot go forward at the pace it should until Telecom Eireann learns some basic home truths. Telecom keeps seeking derogations in Europe whenever this is mentioned, but the reality is that they should have been preparing for deregulation for the last twelve years...The cost of leased lines, which are leased by Telecom Eireann to Esat and others, went up by 500 per cent between 1991 and 1996. It's killing business across the country and it's effectively killing long distance calls. Do we need Telecom at all?"

O'Brien realises the dynamics of the telecommunications industry and the need for players to change as quickly as the technology itself. "Technology is dictating the market. One of Telecom Eireann's pet excuses is that it has a social obligation to provide services to all parts of the country, even the scarcely populated rural areas. But that argument just does not stand up any longer. With technology, you don't have to dig up the roads and lay cables anymore; small transmitters can be bought off the shelf in the US which will do the job."

In spite of many of his criticisms, O'Brien remains optimistic about Ireland's entrepreneurial potential. He cites Irish entrepreneurial successes abroad as examples of how we can thrive even in today's competitive world. He cites our food successes in Eastern Europe where, for example, Avonmore currently controls one third of the milk pool in Budapest. Similarly, he believes that Bord na Mona's acquisition of a distribution base in France was an astute move.

He finishes, however, with another well placed criticism. "But we have to shed some of our inherited baggage. For example in the Czech Republic, thirty-six per cent of employment is in the public service, while in Ireland it is still over thirty per cent, and they have just come out of forty years of communism. Our public sector has to be more commercially focused in its thinking. The head of the New Zealand Central Bank has a performance clause in his salary contract, which is dictated by a number of economic performance factors. These notions are completely alien to us in Ireland."

Because such notions are gospel to Denis O'Brien and the other young entrepreneurial Turks of corporate Ireland, the outlook for our common, corporate future must be promising.

CASE STUDY – HURRAH FOR PADDYWOOD

The billion dollar success of Disney's *The Lion King* and *The Little Mermaid* – made in 1989 and which to date has been a US$4 billion earner – has resulted in substantial salary hikes for animators. Not, alas, for Irish animators! The IDA dream of establishing a 'Cartoon Hollywood' in Ireland ended in November 1995 when Screen Animation, the former Sullivan Bluth and Don Bluth animation studios, closed. Massive redundancies immediately followed.

The IDA misjudged cost trends in this market. Basically, the studios for traditional type animation have returned to Hollywood. Although there is still some piece-work in Ireland and mainland Europe for artists in advertising and multimedia, Disney is once again supreme in full length animated feature movies. The IDA had hoped that Disney would open an Irish studio when it was looking at European locations. Disney decided otherwise. As a sector for creating value-added employment, the IDA's policy ultimately bombed.

The IDA attempt to set up a cartoon movie industry came just as the major Hollywood studios slashed costs by sending drawings to be hand-coloured by low paid workers based in the third world. Overnight, Irish studios were under-priced out of the market. Now much of the movement and colouring can be completed by computer scanning programmes which work from basic drawings. The fledgling Irish cartoon industry is, in other words, strategically outmanoeuvred, nearly as dead as the dodos they had hoped to draw.

In retrospect, the IDA's foray into the movies has been an expensive fiasco. Screen Animation, under various owners and *nommes de guerres*, has gobbled up more than US$100 million in investors' money since it was first established as Sullivan Bluth in 1986. We have nothing but hefty bills to show for it.

Although Don Bluth – the entrepreneur who founded the company, now works for Fox Animation, a subsidiary of Rupert Murdoch's News Corporation – others, including almost all Irish entrepreneurs associated with these glamour projects, have had their fingers burnt to greater degrees than have the main players.

MKB, the Dutch backers of the original venture, invested almost US$50 million before the company went into liquidation in 1992 with the loss of 350 jobs. The company was revived in a joint operation between John Boorman's Merlin Films and Media Assets of Hong Kong. The company was renamed Don Bluth Ireland and three films, in various stages of production at the time of liquidation, were completed.

Although Media Assets had held a majority on the board, they were eventually taken over by News Corporation which invested a further US$60 million in the ultimately doomed project. Merlin eventually sold its interest to News Corporation. These big names and big investments only postponed the fateful day. Hollywood ensured that the project, recklessly spurred on as it was by the twin engines of the IDA's comparative inexperience in this area and the rather more frantic need for a 'success' by our more colourful politicians, was doomed.

Among the films made by the Sullivan Bluth animators were *An American's Tale*, *Thumbelina* and *A Troll In Central Park*. These films never achieved the box office successes of Disney Cartoon films, like *The Lion King*. Nor could they, without special arrangements for preferential distributive rights within the key US market.

Undeterred by this fiasco, recent tax driven plans have striven to promote Ireland as an international film-making centre. Further fiascos have inevitably followed. Michael D Higgins' section 35 preferential tax ruling, designed to re-animate the corpse of the Irish film industry, has created more than its share of controversy. *Space Truckers*, *Sign of the Fish* and *Driftwood* are amongst the funded movies that have found themselves in troubled waters.

Deadwood II Ltd was set up to raise section 35 money for *Space Truckers*. All cheques for investment in the section 35 fund for Deadwood II were made payable to the solicitors. However, almost £1 million of investors' funds were used to fund an entirely different film, *Driftwood*, a psychological thriller which, like *Space Truckers*, was due to be produced by Mary Breen-Farrelly, one of our more colourful film producers.

A further £1.2 million was routed through other companies connected to Breen-Farrelly or her partner John Avery of Oblique Financial Services. These companies included The Choice Ltd, which was producing a ten part animation series, *The Sign of the Fish. The Sign of the Fish* remains unfinished while *Driftwood* had a very difficult birth and was not a financial success. Little, if any, returns are now expected from these ventures.

Expected returns from these mega-hyped glamour events have certainly not been realised! Upto 280 investors put £4 million into Deadwood II Ltd but it now must seem unlikely that they will get their money back.

The funding of *Space Truckers* hit difficulties in summer 1995 and Michael Higgins' Department of Arts, Culture and The Gaeltacht took the interesting step of sanctioning a second section 35 company to allow further investment in the project. Legal difficulties concerning rights to the proceeds of these films have eventuated. While *Space Truckers* did enjoy some financial success when it came out on video, the original investors who put money in when Mary Breen-Farrelly was producing it, have no real chance of getting their money back.

These expensive eye openers raise the question as to how a small country like Ireland can, despite our pipe dreams, hope to compete against larger countries, the USA in particular, which have the technical expertise, economies of scale and distributive networks to guarantee themselves an almost textbook case in world monopoly in this prestige industry which has always been so alluring to the proud, stupid and gullible.

Ireland was not the first to wantonly try to crack Hollywood's hegemony and Higgins was not the first politician to get the brainwave that there was "money in movies". The British and Australian movie industries, for example, have tried and failed. *The Mission*, a British film which scooped scores of international awards, lost a fortune and set the British film industry back a decade. *Crocodile Dundee*, *The Man From Snowy River* and *Mad Max* apart, few Australian movies have made it to financial success abroad.

If Britain and Australia find it difficult to compete, what chance has little, under resourced Ireland? They, at least, have some critical mass on which to found an industry. We have none. On one hand, there is a shortage of trained Irish camera crews to do whatever work is available in good times and, on the other hand, there is not enough casual work to see them over the dry patches between movies. Much of the £20 million a year of tax payers' money given to the movie industry by former Arts Minister Michael D Higgins has, in fact, more often than not merely created temporary employment for foreign film technicians who move to Ireland for short periods of highly paid work.

In 1994, £133 million, of which £51 million was raised locally, was invested in sixty-one film projects shot wholly or in part in Ireland. Tax rebates of about £20 million were also forthcoming. Few, if any, full-time jobs emerged. The part-time jobs that did emerge worked out as the equivalent of 1,300 full-time jobs – at a cost of almost £16,000 each per annum – significantly higher than comparable figures quoted in this book.

Tinseltown's potential for developing the Irish film industry has to be assessed in the context of what it has cost the exchequer, and what has been gained for that cost. In 1994/95, section 35 funding raised £42 million. During this period the exchequer impact of section 35 funded projects amounted to a net loss to the exchequer of just under £4 million: a benefit of £15.86 million offset by a cost of £19.4 million.

Section 35 movies have been almost exclusively tax driven. More than thirty-two per cent of section 35 films would not have been produced at all, without the existence of this scheme: perhaps most of these should not have been made at all. However, forty per cent of productions would have been made outside Ireland, while forty-four per cent of film producers have said, in surveys, that without the scheme they would have employed a lower level of Irish staff on the production.

Now that so much investors' money has bolted, the padlocks have been applied to this scheme. The 1996 budget presaged a serious crackdown in the way it was operated. New measures were introduced to ensure the exchequer gets better value for the haemorrhage in tax revenues which the scheme has caused.

A number of major obstacles still stand in the way of developing the sector to meet the challenges ahead. The industry is still very project-based and, as ever, we lack the necessary economies of scale to effectively compete. There remains a limited pool of senior talent, while crew shortages and labour market inflexibilities are all too prevalent.

The changes in the operation of the scheme led to less multi-million pound films coming to Ireland. *Braveheart*, *Michael Collins* and *Space Truckers* may not be replicated. Perhaps this will be a good thing and it will force our leaders to address similar glamorous industries in a more sober fashion than they have been wont to do in the past.

Financial intermediaries and financiers will also have to re-examine the Irish film investment market in the light of these changing circumstances. Film investment, through section 35, is not now as attractive as it was. Ultimately, although the smaller indigenous film industry will benefit, Paddywood will remain the expensive pipe dream that it always was.

If only our leaders could heed the obvious, here as much as elsewhere! A special report, commissioned by the Departments of Finance and Arts Culture and The Gaeltacht, was compiled by an Indecon economist, Alan Gray, and submitted to the Departments before Christmas 1995. This was to form the backbone of their analysis of the impact of section 35 and the potential for the film industry. Although this report made twenty-four recommendations, only seven of them were adopted. Among the recommendations were the establishment of a Screen Commission and modifications to corporate tax rules to facilitate the generation of profitable film companies in Ireland. Gray also recommended that industrial development agencies should pursue strategies to encourage Irish film companies to develop scale and upgrade strategic management resources.

These reforms could have included the provision of selective employment grants and the use of mentor and patron programmes. These proposals were canned. So were more urgent ones!

One of the most urgent of these canned recommendations was that the industry should urgently enter consultations with the trade unions to address the issue of market entry restrictions and inflexibility in labour market practices. As Gray commented: "State incentives which simply cushion an industry from addressing lack of competitiveness or inflexible practices represents a waste of scarce taxpayer resources and also damages the long term sustainability of the industry." In Arts, as in everywhere else, the government felt it more important to protect the vested interests of their supporters than to actually govern.

If Ireland is to have even the most modest of sustainable film industries, it must come up with bankable projects in either of our official national languages. Projects, designed merely to subsidise pet projects or to give employment to the favoured but talentless few with access to the correct ears will have to be discontinued. Other shady practices in the Arts industry will also have to be eradicated. The whole Arts sector claims to have generated a gross annual revenue of some £450 million in recent years; it claims to directly employ about 21,500 people full-time equivalents, accounting for 2.4 per cent of total employment; the Arts Council has calculated its minimum export value at a whopping £100 million.

The Arts Council estimates that it needs £26 million annually, to contribute to Ireland's economic and cultural growth. Their arguments, which centre around the need to pump more taxpayers' money into kick-starting a more general interest in their pet projects, seem economically specious at best. Even as the leisure industry increases internationally, it is doubtful that, in infrastructurally-starved Ireland, it can be a solid foundation stone for future growth. We cannot step-dance our way out of recession!

That said, entertainment is a definite growth area where Ireland has something to offer an international audience. The *Riverdance* spectacle has become a multi-national, multi-million pound industry in its own right. Rock tours and the rock tourism industry are both booming. Denis Desmond's MCD Management Services controls about seventy-five per cent of the major touring groups coming to Ireland. He owns the SFX and has interests in the Tivoli, the Columbia Mills, the River Club and the Olympia Theatre. His turnover of about £14 million a year makes him a major Irish player. New forms of tourism aimed at the young could be developed if official Ireland would get off its collective butt and work closer with the likes of Denis Desmond.

The potential is clearly there. Records by Irish stars like U2, the Cranberries and Daniel O'Donnell are now proportionately outselling traditional Irish food and drink exports in Germany, Britain and other key European markets. Although the success of Irish music is attributable to the talent of the country's composers, performers, publishers and producers, greater State assistance is necessary to allow the industry to grow. IBEC believes that tax-based incentives, such as those pertaining in the film industry, would benefit the industry greatly. Leaving aside the argument that tax subsidies unduly distort the market, IBEC believes that a properly structured music industry could, in time, create an additional 15,000 jobs and generate another £300 million of exports within the next decade. IBEC says that an overhaul of the copyright laws, the elimination of VAT on cassettes and CDs and further support structures for music industry investors are needed if the industry's full potential is to be realised.

IBEC's music industry body points out the obvious: that the music sector, which currently employs 10,000 people directly and has exports worth in excess of £160 million, lacks the required infrastructure to avail of market opportunities. It also points out that technological advances make it increasingly susceptible to piracy. To counter this threat, IBEC advocates home recording royalties on blank tapes to compensate artists, publishers and record companies for losses through private copying which it maintains is worth a further £7 million a year. They also want to see the 1963 Copyright Act revamped.

Although IBEC's proposals may be criticised for containing no strategy for growth but for instead merely looking for increased tax breaks for their members, those in the music business in this instance, they have at least shown the vibrancy and potential of this sector.

CHAPTER FOUR

Services Ireland

Services now account for the largest share of employment and virtually all of the employment growth in developed countries. Services comprise less than ten per cent of our exports, compared to an EU average of over twenty per cent. Irish public policy continues to pay far more attention to the manufacturing and primary production sectors than to services development, a possible cornerstone to our future economic viability.

The further growth of our services offers us a number of advantages that may not be so easy to achieve elsewhere in our economy. The services sector is generally labour-intensive, thus, output growth in services, will generally contribute more than other sectors to employment levels. Further, because of lower capital requirements in comparison with other sectors of economic activity, economies of scale tend to be of less importance and barriers to entry correspondingly weaker here than in the more traditional industrial sector. For these reasons, employment in the services sector may respond quicker to more correctly-focused policy changes than other sectors can. Our case studies, by showing how easy it is to enter these markets and what the rewards can be like for those who develop them over time, exemplify these points.

CASE STUDY – DAVID MCKENNA'S MARLBOROUGH INTERNATIONAL

Successful Irish entrepreneurs have had few things in common in the past. But one thing they tended to share was the maxim, stay away from the stock exchange. Because our stock exchange was small, conservative and we lacked a major share-buying culture, many of our most successful entrepreneurs kept their businesses in private hands. It was also part of the culture to keep all of your financial matters personal and private, or amongst family, given that many of our successful indigenous companies were family-owned.

That has changed dramatically in the last few years. The Irish Stock Exchange can claim a number of recent entrepreneurial successes. One of the most recent and successful flotations on our Stock Exchange was the recruitment group, Marlborough International. The company floated in Autumn 1997 at a share price of 96p. By the end of May 1998 it was trading at 340p, with a market capitalisation of over £100m, and earning profits of over £3m.

The success of Marlborough is largely attributable to the efforts and business acumen of one man, its managing director, David McKenna. But when you talk to him about the success of the company, he will always attribute it to the quality of the people he has around him. Having bought the company out of receivership only few years ago for £6,000, McKenna's shares are now worth on paper over £50m.

Marlborough's main activity is in the general recruitment and placement of personnel on permanent, temporary and short-term contracts with a broad spread of companies. Currently Marlborough is placing 1,400 people per week in work. In Ireland it has offices in Dublin, Waterford, Cork, Limerick and Galway, with plans to open more, including Sligo.

It has two principal operating subsidiaries, Marlborough Group Ltd and Professional Placement Group Ltd. The Marlborough name accounts for about seventy per cent of the group's total fee income. McKenna bought it from a receiver in 1991 and relaunched it in 1992. McKenna's tenacity in turning into the company it is today, should be acknowledged, yet when asked about whether he has always been entrepreneurial, he answers "no".

"I left school at 15. And all I wanted was to get an apprenticeship. I got my apprenticeship as a plumber and took it from there. People talk about the role of education in facilitating entrepreneurship, but I went to school in Tallaght, and frankly, some days you would be taught and some day you wouldn't."

McKenna emigrated with his qualification as a plumber and found that he was making good money in Algeria, installing plumbing and heating. In the late 1980s he went to Britain, where he set up a sprinkler installation business. This was probably his first taste of running his own business. He found that in a relatively short period of time, he was making money and placing people in contract work in that sector and then in the construction sector in general.

When he returned to Ireland he got directly involved in the recruitment industry. "I started sourcing people for the construction industry in England. It was ironic that in those days I was in Ireland, trying to find suitable work for people in England. Now I find myself in Ireland trying to source people in England and other places to come back and work here."

It is also ironic that after a short while back in Ireland he offered to buy Marlborough, but he was told that it was not for sale and it wouldn't be, according to McKenna. The company later went into receivership and he bought it for £6,000. McKenna steadily built it up to what it is today. But at that time in 1991, did he ever envisage that it would be so successful? Was he making a clever move based on his assessment of how the economy and recruitment business was about to go?

"I knew from the construction industry, the importance of contract work, and the idea of out-sourcing. I could see from the foreign multi-nationals, especially those from the US, that this was the way they tended to operate. I suppose I could also see that with a larger number of foreign companies coming in, there would be a demand for this kind of service."

"As the company began to grow, we came to an invoice discounting arrangement with AIB, and that made a huge difference to the business. It really helped us through a number of years."

"I really realised for the first time that the business had a lot of potential in February 1997, when I was offered over stg£17m to sell the business. It really dawned on me then for the first time." To many people, who are not entrepreneurs, the idea of turning down an offer of £17m and enjoying the money for the rest of your life seems odd. But McKenna had other ideas.

"Sure I could have accepted the offer and taken the money. But I was thirty-five years old. What was I going to do for the rest of my life, other than use the money to start all over again? I decided also that because I was surrounded by really good people in Marlborough, who worked so hard to make it what it was, that I shouldn't just sell. At that point I decided to investigate the possibility of floating the company on the Stock Exchange."

Today, Marlborough continues to grow as part of an ever-growing economy. The backdrop to its expansion has been favourable, with a number of factors coming right for the Irish economy over this period including demographics, EU transfers, foreign direct investment and buoyant domestic demand. In addition, the trend towards out-sourcing the recruitment function especially in the area of contract labour, the gradual shift in employment trends to more part-time and contract work and the technology boom have all served to increase activity in the recruitment sector.

Overall net fee income has risen dramatically over the last few years from £2.1 million in the year to February 1995 to £4.6 million for the year to the end of February 1997. Marlborough employs over sixty consultants and is the leading general recruitment company in Ireland by a significant margin. It focuses on providing computing/IT, technical, commercial, secretarial and contract personnel for most industry sectors. The contracts division of the group has over 800 contract staff on its payroll. Currently this division is devoted to providing an outsourcing recruitment service to the high profile multi-nationals including Dell, Motorola, KAO among others.

Its key skills are the maintenance of a candidate database of 80,000 CV's (35,000 computerised). This enables the company to provide a quick and comprehensive response to client enquiries and has greatly assisted the company in gaining a high percentage of the high volume contracts tendered for over the last year.

The company has built a solid platform, from which it can benefit further, assuming the economic outlook remains positive. A variety of factors continue to work to its advantage. Favourable demographic trends, macro-economic stability, strong foreign direct investment and buoyant domestic demand are among the many factors underpinning above average economic growth in Ireland over the next few years.

One key determinant of an economy's capacity to grow is the growth in the labour force. Over the past five years, the Irish labour force has risen on average by 2.2% per year. The total workforce ha risen by a cumulative 250,000 this decade. This contrasts sharply with the average EU experience. Similarly, foreign direct investment has played a major role, and that looks set to continue.

Irish-based multi-nationals have been out-sourcing many activities traditionally done in-house and this had led to the increased use of contract labour. Indigenous companies are also increasing their use of contract labour. Elsewhere, the IT boom is fuelling the demand for specialist IT consultants. Recruitment companies are acting as agents for these self-employed consultants. The millennium and Euro issues should sustain this trend for some time yet, certainly to beyond the year 2000.

McKenna is bullish about the future for the economy in general and his company in particular. All of the economic projections point towards good growth for his business. However, any downturn in the economy is likely to be felt early on, by his sector. McKenna believes you can only prepare for a possible downturn, in terms of how to react to it, but there is nothing you can do about it. "We are prepared for any possible downturn. I think that given the way the sector in Ireland is so fragmented, we could improve our market share in a downturn, although profit growth would suffer." His sector is highly fragmented, with 270 issued recruitment licences. Many of these companies employ only about two or three people. While there are no market share figures for the industry in Ireland, and only estimates of its size, McKenna estimates that the sector is worth about £200 million per year.

He has clearly made it as an entrepreneur, but he is not sure how society can legislate to increase the number of entrepreneurs. "In terms of education, for example, I do not see how you can teach someone to be an entrepreneur. It is something they have or they don't. Those who have it will just do it, unless something specific gets in their way. Our educational standards are very high and I'm not sure how they could be changed to make them more entpreneurial."

Part of the problem in Ireland has been that we have good managers but no enough good entrepreneurs – what is the difference. For McKenna, the entrepreneur is the one who will push the boat out that bit further. For example, he points out that we have a lot of good managers in Ireland who run businesses very well. Similarly we have a lot of people who can start up a business and make it profitable. But once they reach a certain size and the attain a certain semi-comfortable lifestyle, they don't want to go on an expand. They are not willing to risk everything to turn it into something bigger.

McKenna argues that the fortune he has made does not seriously effect him and his lifestyle. "I work harder now than I did before. In terms of the good life, I enjoyed a good life before I floated the company, and I enjoy a good life now."

One of the obstacles to creating a more vibrant culture has been the banks, according to McKenna. He believes they have been too conservative when it came to lending out money to prospective entrepreneurs. "If you do not have track record they do not want to know you. If you run into financial trouble in Ireland, you will go bust. But then again, you probably have to go bust once to really understand business and know what its all about. Five or six years ago, you could borrow from the banks, but they really charged you high rates of interest on the basis that you were a risk. We are in a position to get very good rates of interest now because of our position and our track record, but a few years ago you had to pay a lot higher. But the introduction of invoice discounting was big help for us."

On a policy level, the reductions in corporation tax will deliver the kind of increased profit levels and jobs that have been promised by the business community. "Its good to see the government taking this issue more seriously. There has been the crazy situation of companies going to the bank to borrow money to pay their corporation tax and it just got them into difficulties."

The fact that the Irish Stock Exchange has really taken off, and we are now approaching a share-buying culture, is also seen as a good thing by McKenna. "There are more punters out there. Traditionally a lot of the good businesses in Ireland were family-owned, and in that kind of situation it is difficult to make decisions. This did not facilitate the flotation of family-owned businesses on the stock market. In our case it made a lot of sense, because it gave us the access to the finance we needed to expand the business."

Since flotation, McKenna has been busy on the expansion front. Earlier this year Marlborough bought Walker Hamill, a British recruitment business for stg£17m. McKenna has recently been to Australia and back to Britain, and possibly two more acquisitions are expected soon.

What is clear from talking to McKenna, is that he will continue to pursue the expansion of his business with a view to becoming a major international player. By making international acquisitions he is also safeguarding the performance of the group, if there is an economic downturn in Ireland. Furthermore, by expanding internationally, he is exporting his own services industry expertise abroad. As we pointed out, the services industry providing a huge percentage of our new indigenous jobs, but few Irish entrepreneurs have managed to build international service companies. Another businessman who has managed to move in that direction is Ray Kearns.

CASE STUDY – RAY KEARNS' RE-ENGINEERING OF IRISH EDUCATION

Ray Kearns set up the Dublin Institute of Education, because he recognised the potential demand here for private education. Originally from Ballaghaderreen in County Roscommon, Kearns left his home in the West to work for CIE on the North Wall in Dublin, where he also studied at night for his Leaving Cert. Ray knew that he could do better and so, after a hard day's work, he would knuckle down to the books. Kearns describes the completion of his Leaving Cert as his entrance into the corridor of real opportunity; it enabled him to pursue a working life which would otherwise have been denied him. His horizons broadened.

Shortly after the introduction of free education, Kearns began offering private education from his base in Leeson Street. At a time when people could study in the evenings and on weekends for virtually nothing, through the VEC, Kearns was charging for similar courses. "People thought I was crazy trying to sell education. Why would students pay for a service which they could get somewhere else for nothing? My results showed them why."

Kearns is insistent that the credit for his success is as much due to good fortune and circumstance as to his own endeavours. "You can build the proverbial better mouse-trap if you will. You can put together an educational product that is second to none but if the circumstances are not right, no matter how well prepared you are, you more than likely won't succeed. When opportunity knocks you must be prepared to avail of it." In his own case, he instances the circumstances of Ireland in the early 1970s which allowed him to develop his business. "The late Donough O'Malley opened up the educational sluice-gates. He brought in free education which, coupled with the post-war baby boom, meant that there was a huge upsurge in students sitting the Leaving Cert. O'Malley also introduced the points system for entry to university so it became more important for students wishing to enter university to do better in their Leaving Certs. Coupled with these developments was the new maths with which even many of the maths teachers had trouble. The schools were caught in a dilemma. I had caught an opportunity that I was almost uniquely qualified in terms of education, personal character and motivation to capitalise on."

To back up this claim, Kearns explains how, despite seemingly overwhelming odds, he got to the stage where he could benefit from the changes O'Malley implemented. "The North Wall was hard. We worked from 2pm to 10pm every day with only a twenty minute lunch break. However, I had the motivation to better myself and so, despite putting in a hard day's work, I studied for my Leaving Cert and got into UCD on the basis of my results. I suffered the embarrassment of having to pay my fees by instalment. I was certainly not aware of any fellow student who was so hard up that they had to pay as they went. Even then, despite the odds, I knew I could go further." As evidence of this, Kearns cites his achievement in being elected by an overall majority of the students as President of the Students' Council. He regarded his victory achieved, in part, by canvassing students his rivals ignored, as a further vindication of his basic contention that application, tenacity and hard work do pay off.

After leaving UCD, Kearns was awarded a scholarship to the University of Pittsburgh where he got an MA in the New Mathematics and where he saw private enterprise at work in its American setting. "America was pivotal in showing me what could be done. I then returned to Ireland and was appointed senior maths master at the Jesuit-run Gonzaga College. Again, the urge to succeed remained strong and so I started to provide private tuition for other students at rooms I rented in Rosse's College. Although conditions were basic, the students got the results they wanted and gradually business picked up. Because I also gave classes to my fellow teachers for the Department of Education, I became more and more familiar with the needs of the educational industry I had worked so hard to get into. Whilst I was becoming more knowledgeable about the intricacies of the industry, I continued to work hard and because my students got such good results, the word spread that I gave good value for money. In time, I moved to rented accommodation in Lesson Street and, as the business developed, I bought and refurbished the buildings that currently house The Institute of Education."

"All of this came from hard work, a determination to succeed by being the best and by keeping attuned to the needs of the educational sector. The results of my students are there to attest to the effort that has been put into my business."

His results continue to impress. Indeed, some of his teachers, such as Johnny Browne, the maths teacher, have become legends in their own time, such is the standard of their teaching and the consistency of their results. Browne is one of a select coterie who have been with Kearns from the earliest days and, though very many former students would put Browne at top of the class when it comes to teaching, Kearns believes that Johnny Browne typifies a more general quality to be found in his teaching staff. "When I hire new teachers, I generally only consider one burning question: are they the best available? Will they deliver the goods to the students? If they are the best, I want them. It's as simple as that."

The Institute of Education now has over 1,000 students studying for the Leaving Cert on a full-time basis. It also has several hundred more students on part-time courses. "My success shows me that if your product is good enough, it transcends monetary considerations. Despite what others may say, people will vote with their feet and, while we charge for the educational services we are providing, we get our numbers on the basis of what we are selling, and it is something much better than what you can get for nothing elsewhere. Our results continue to prove that quality brings its own rewards."

In conversation, it becomes immediately apparent that Kearns is proud, in the most selfless way, about what he and his students have achieved. He continually returns both to his own Leaving Cert and to the genuine pride and happiness he feels in helping others crack into the corridors of opportunity.

Kearns' business has, in more recent times, successfully expanded to encompass third level education; he is the president and proprietor of Portobello College, Ireland's most successful private university and he is likewise proud of what his former students are now achieving for themselves in the business world. He is also well aware of what he himself has achieved.

He has personally invested over £6 million into the buildings alone, and Portobello, which offers a range of courses, including a three-year degree in Law, awarded by the University of Cardiff, currently has 1,000 students, who typically pay £2,000 per year for a full-time course. When combined with the second level Institute of Education, Kearns estimates that he has the largest private education enterprise of its kind in Europe. He attributes this to the "blood sweat and tears" of himself and his colleagues and to the fact that he believed in the potential for private education in Ireland before others did.

"I saw an opportunity and hammered away at the door until it opened. I am still hammering away, working up to twenty hours a day on occasion. Other doors will, in time, open believe me."

Some doors have been slammed in his face. The decision to abolish all third-level fees for State colleges could potentially fatally damage the third-level sector of Kearns' business. Kearns has launched a legal challenge to this decision, arguing that private education should also be exempted. "This will be a good thing. It will allow us to train those Irish students, who currently have to go abroad for their education. It will allow us to solidify our domestic base and win even more contracts abroad."

Aside from this possible setback, Kearns' businesses are experiencing unprecedented growth. This is largely coming from the high domestic demand for education and the willingness of parents to pay to secure a better future for the their children. Although he believes that this demand will always be there, he has also made significant inroads into the international market, most notably in Malaysia. He has arrangements with three private colleges there whereby he runs Irish Leaving Cert courses for those students wishing to pursue third-level courses here.

"Globally, the trend in education is changing. This is particularly apparent to me when I travel east of Suez. With the Leaving Cert, we are offering a very superior product to buyers in these markets. Some powerful people begrudge me what I am achieving in Asia and elsewhere even though what I am doing is only a drop in the ocean to what the Australians, the Scots and the Canadians are doing. The government should be helping long-established firms like my own. They should not be hindering us."

He is undaunted by the scale of the opposition and, although he has agreements with Irish universities that prospective students will first study for the Leaving Cert in his Institute of Education, he is about to take this arrangement a step further. Kearns has already got clearance from the Department of Education to set up a centre for the Leaving Cert in Malaysia. This would involve Malaysian students studying under Irish teachers, in their own country, for the Irish Leaving Cert. Under the proposed arrangement, the students would sit the exam in Malaysia at the same time it is being sat in Ireland.

"The Irish Leaving Cert is now being increasingly recognised internationally mostly because the English 'A' Level exam has, to some extent, fallen out of favour. Therefore, there is demand for the Leaving Cert on the grounds that it is the best well rounded education available on the international market."

Kearns believes many of these Malaysian students will sit their Leaving Certs over there, and then come to study in our universities. "We have currently 200 students studying for the Leaving Cert in Malaysia. This scheme has enormous potential and we could see it moving to other countries. I'm already exploring opportunities in South Africa."

Vietnam and China are other key markets holding potential for the export of Irish education. He is also making considerable inroads into the lucrative American market and spends a considerable amount of time developing academic links with institutions there. Kearns believes that, while education as a service exported from Ireland holds enormous potential, serious impediments to success remain. Challenging State monopolies is not easy.

Kearns maintains the decision by the former Minister for Education to introduce free fees for State colleges is ultimately short-sighted. "If she was to show insight, she could say that in twenty-five years from now, there may not be the same demand for third-level places. The State could co-operate with the private sector in this regard and could provide for future students without having to undergo the hefty publicly funded capital investment projects that they are currently involved in."

All of these State responses feed into a general dismissiveness of what he has achieved. He believes that there is still a strong tendency in Ireland to vilify the achievements of the entrepreneur. He cites the wealth tax as a begrudgery-inspired piece of legislation which has resulted in over £100 million being squirrelled out of Ireland in recent years by frightened investors.

"Only a miserable fifteen per cent of national income is reinvested in the economy. This is largely due to these high taxes. Until we change our ethos, savings – almost £100 million a week – over one and a half billion pounds a year, each year, will continue to be squirrelled overseas. If these financial haemorrhages could be stopped, domestic investment could bring a multiplier effect with additional returns coming from increased employment, purchasing, sub contracting and the like. The government should be concentrating on fixing these major problems, not taxing local entrepreneurs out of existence."

He further maintains that services have always got something of a raw deal in Ireland. "Our services industries have not been treated with the respect they deserve. I think things are beginning to be seen in a different light. I am long enough established to be afforded respect in terms of what has been achieved." Kearns is quick to point out that the children of his staunchest critics very often attended courses in his centres.

There is a reluctance by the State sector to accept competition as a major obstacle impeding not only his own efforts but those of other entrepreneurs as well. "It should be written into the constitution that no one, least of all the inept, should have a monopoly of any kind. There is no substitute for healthy competition."

Kearns sees Ireland's long-term future resting in developing critical comparative advantages. In this context he sees huge potential for tourism, as well as services like education. Like Denis Brosnan of the Kerry Group, he also believes in keeping successful Irish businesses in Irish hands for as long as possible. While accepting that many Irish companies will have to sell out in order for the business to grow and develop in international markets, he also sees education as something of an exception. Kearns is confident of handing on his business to his children, and maintains he will never sell it. Some would argue that his operation is ripe to be floated on the Stock Exchange or to be sold off to an educational multi-national. But Kearns says those issues will be decided by the next generation, and not by him. He is confident of handing on to his children the multi-million pound business he built up whilst working on the North Wall and studying part-time for his Leaving Cert.

CASE STUDY – SELLING OURSELVES ABROAD

If Kearns' ambitions are to be fully realised, we will have to change many of our pre-conceptions. In particular, we will have to increasingly regard education and similar services as tradeable commodities. George Kiely, regional manager of the Overseas Development Department with the Irish Trade Board, believes the export of Irish services is a crucial component in guaranteeing our future national well-being.

Having gained over eleven years valuable experience with the Trade Board in places as diverse as Iraq and Singapore, Kiely maintains that Irish education is already highly valued abroad. "This is something which can be worked on. I don't believe there are any problems in finding the markets to export education. It's more of a problem with re-engineering the structures at home than it is in finding suitable markets."

"Although, in the past, Ireland might have been criticised as being rather lethargic in selling our educational expertise around the world, we are now getting the desired results. For example, the Irish Management Institute (IMI) has set up a course on entrepreneurial development with a Malaysian government agency. They plan to export the course around south-east Asia."

Irish marketing expertise has also been successfully exported. Irish consultants have won contracts to assist in setting up trade boards similar to Ireland's in twenty-six countries. Singapore, one of these countries, even models the office lay-out of the Singapore Trade Board on its counterpart in Dublin!

Kiely believes there is further considerable potential in exporting consultancy services in Eastern Europe. He points to the semi-State concept which has emerged in Ireland. "Eastern European countries like the idea of the semi-State company. As countries coming out of communist regimes, it is like a midway house between State and private ownership. They need these types of organisations which, though not directly part of the government, help to maintain social stability."

But how, given the breadth and depth of competition, can Irish management and financial consultants hope to be able to compete for major contracts in a global playing field? Kiely maintains that our successes as an export-driven country give us a valuable edge over many of our competitors. "We are the largest exporter per capita in the world. For countries like those in Eastern Europe or Vietnam, we are seen as a former colony which has emerged to become a very successful exporter of goods and services. We are respected and emulated."

Kiely, in fact, further argues that Irish consultants are highly valued not only in developing countries but also in Brussels, where they get a significantly higher number of consultancy contracts than do their competitors. He also argues that the development of our international services sector could provide our graduates with valuable experience before returning home with the benefit of that experience. He especially emphasises the potential for financial consultancy in this regard. "There are a lot of one man operations out there in the consultancy business. It would be much more beneficial to semi-institutionalise or formalise these to get greater aggregate returns." Kiely believes that the institutional biases in favour of exporting manufacturing goods will have to be modified until we can guarantee more long-term supply and logistical back up.

To support his argument, he recounts his experiences in Baghdad when he personally arranged the sale of £17 million worth of Irish goods in one year to Iraq. He cites one example of a Middle Eastern clothes distribution group which told him it was interested in buying Western style wedding dresses. He duly sourced one Irish wedding dress manufacturer and brought back a few samples. The Middle Eastern buyers ordered £1 million worth of dresses, which trebled the Irish company's workforce for six months. He recounts how, during the Iran/Iraq War, vast amounts of Carroll's cigarettes, Power's Whiskey and Irish electrical goods were sold in Baghdad. Kiely also says that the Iraqis were particularly attracted to the idea of a whiskey being called Power and uses this example to convincingly argue how, unless the brands can take hold in the market, consumer goods will eventually be sourced from countries where they can be manufactured more cheaply with lower labour costs.

"During my time in Iraq, we made Carroll's the number one seller. The brand name helped immensely. Iraqis use the phrase number one a lot: your number one taxi driver, number one secretary, number one waiter are all saying that they are the best at what they do. They will therefore smoke the number one cigarette which, of course, was Carroll's Number One, what else?"

Kiely points to another viable strategy. He notes how Irish companies have been quite successful in supplying Irish-based branches of the major multi-national companies. Kiely argues that this form of subcontracting can also be exported. He points to the example of the Kerry Group, which is supplying ingredients to multi-national food groups in the Far East. "There is no reason why more Irish supply companies cannot go down this route. We have to realise just how small the domestic market is and find profitable markets elsewhere." Kiely, as befitting a member of the Irish Diaspora, has spent many years outside of Ireland. Born in Liverpool and educated in London, he maintains that there is a vast Irish network spanning the globe, waiting to be tapped into. "Ireland must tap into the rich resources of her diaspora, in Liverpool as much as anywhere else. They must harness the experiences of the diaspora to our common advantage. Scousers (people raised in Liverpool) are, for example, born to sell. They get out and hustle. That is their culture. They are confident and believe in the product they are selling. Not everybody can do it. Ireland must tap into the abilities, not only of Mersey-siders, but of those world-wide who feel part of the wider Irish family."

Although Kiely admits that not everybody is a natural seller, he praises the achievements of Tony Courtney, Jim Mongey and his other colleagues, who have achieved very much with limited resources. He believes that the Irish, because they are prepared to foot slog, can achieve results superior to their competitors. "International selling is not the romantic story Hollywood might make it out to be. It is a long, hard, mostly hidden slog, where you might have to wait patiently for up to a week for a meeting that might then be postponed. You must deal with and respect the various cultures you meet. This comes naturally to many of us. From my youngest days in Liverpool to my time working for the Trade Board in Mexico and Singapore, I have found tremendous goodwill for the Irish at all levels of all societies. Although the international networking skills of Tony O'Reilly and our other top rank entrepreneurs are there for all to see, ABT are busy nurturing links wherever the Irish can be found. These days, that means every conceivable place on the earth's surface. We at ABT are also there, pushing the cause of Irish business."

Clearly then, as the advantages which sustained us in former days vanish, others appear for those of us willing and able to avail of them. However, these new approaches must be founded on a fundamental reassessment and consequent reappraisal of many of our prevailing notions about marketing and the marketplace. Our comparative advantages would seem to lie as much in ourselves as they do in any other more quantifiable resources that we might have. The same applies to tourism, our biggest service sector earner.

CASE STUDY – TOURIST DOLLARS

International tourism is growing at four per cent per annum. Irish tourism is expected to grow significantly faster. Key drivers for growth include the trend away from sun holidays, the upward trend in special interest holidays, the peace and the perception of Ireland as a cultural, musical and recreational alternative to mainland European destinations.

We currently get over four million overseas visitors a year. A strong performance in the North American, Australasian and Japanese markets, together with double digit growth from Britain and mainland Europe, looks set to yield us a credible increase in overseas visitor expenditure. The contribution made to the economy by tourism is set to overtake agriculture.

Britain, which provides us with a £500 million revenue from tourism, remains our most important market. Mainland European visitors spend £425 million a year, whilst visitors from Australasia account for a further £88 million in tourist revenue.

Although the years ahead should see this healthy trend continue, there are potential down sides as well. An increasing proportion of holiday traffic consists of short lead time supplementary holiday breaks; any notable lessening of cost competitiveness would swiftly have a traumatic effect on this vital industry.

As in any comparable industry, if we wish to capitalise on our popularity, we must make major inputs in time, money and effort. Although the Irish have several strengths in this area, based on our non-quantifiable traits of openness and friendliness, we also have more quantifiable weaknesses. Ireland is an expensive, poorly-marketed destination with bad transport facilities and major gaps in the few facilities we offer the discerning visitor. Given that European tourists tend towards more individualised, less-packaged holidays than our more traditional tourists, reform is essential.

While the Irish tourism industry has shown phenomenal growth, and it has risen to that challenge very well, it still remains seriously underdeveloped. Although revenues from tourism have increased measurably there is, as our US case study exemplifies, scope for much more accelerated growth. Ireland's net gain from tourism is, at present, less than two per cent of GNP. When we consider that over fifty per cent of tourists to Ireland from the US, come here to visit relatives or to trace their roots, our potential for profitable expansion becomes apparent.

Estimating the employment and GNP contribution of tourism is a notoriously complex task. Tourism is not a precisely defined industry: rather it is a disparate collection of goods and services. Because locals share the facilities which tourists enjoy, it is difficult to get precise figures of the value-added component of tourism. Because of its seasonal nature, profit is less dependable than in non-seasonal sectors and proper marketing is that bit more difficult. These problems are not unique to Ireland.

Subject to these constraints, a proper tourism policy has much to offer. Apart from its national implications in terms of foreign exchange earnings and employment, tourism has a very important regional dimension in that the gains generally flow disproportionately to regions with below average incomes. Tourism receipts, in other words, tend to be higher in regions with low incomes per head. Ireland's western regions, for example, though they contain only thirty-eight per cent of our population, receive fifty-three per cent of our tourism income. But the fact that Dublin has enjoyed a large percentage of the recent growth in tourism revenue, further heightens the regional issue.

The kingdom of Kerry exemplifies this point. Kerry's tourism industry could undoubtedly provide extra sustenance and opportunities for many more Kerry people. However, keeping competition out, even at the expense of capping growth well below its sustainable level, remains the main objective of many of the players currently in this field. There is no reason why they should risk expansion for increased taxation. Their well founded fears result in stagnation and retardation. Strategic, workable plans whereby, for example, tourist events could become greater revenue earners for a greater number of people, need extra infrastructure. To take but one example: there is an obvious shortage of major hotels in all of south Kerry and so south Kerry-based tours cannot achieve sustainable and viable volume.

Given its peripheral position, the south-west, to survive let alone thrive, must concentrate, *inter alia*, on tourism. Financial incentives, to encourage the upgrading of airports, hotels, fishing facilities and related infrastructure, must be forthcoming. The nubs and the entrepreneurship already exist. Faranfore, which is privately-owned and privately funded, has a major role to play in this. Organised commuting between Faranfore and nearby Shannon airport can only do both good.

Although tourism can provide a much needed rural boost, the south-western corridor highlights the structural and other constraints that Ireland as a nation labours under. The economy is built on tiny, microbe like firms, too small and too unempowered to overly concern our unions and government policy-makers. Clearly, more volume is needed to avail of the opportunities which our case study of the lucrative US market makes plain, are there in abundance. Americans are attracted to Europe because of our cultural and leisure attractions. Cost considerations are becoming increasingly important to Americans in determining their choice of airlines and hotels.

US international holidaymakers, and particularly those who travel to long haul destinations, tend to be older, better off and better educated than the US population as a whole. The long haul holiday maker is very likely to be over forty-five and travelling with a partner. Retired folk comprise over a quarter of those who make trips to Europe.

Although not as pre-eminent as they were in the 1980s, US holiday makers are extremely valuable to the Irish tourist industry. They have a higher propensity to spend than do the Europeans, their needs are, in general, easier to identify, and so, despite recent set backs, there is much scope for increasing trans-Atlantic volume.

Like all other markets, this one must be carefully nurtured. Only twenty-two million Americans, thirteen per cent of the American adult population, hold passports. However, this thirteen per cent spend about $55 billion per annum on international travel. This makes them the world's biggest travel spenders.

About forty-five million trips are taken by US residents to destinations outside the US each year; just under half of these involve air travel. The countries most visited are those, such as Mexico and Canada, which lie in the immediate ambit of the US. About sixty per cent of our American holidaymakers make their own independent arrangements when visiting here; a further sixteen per cent come here on fully inclusive tours and a further twenty-five per cent pre-purchase land arrangements through the travel trade.

Although Americans tend to spread themselves out whilst here, Dublin, Kerry and the Shannon region remain their most popular haunts.

Golf, cycling, angling and, of course, genealogical tracing are our most popular draw cards.

US tourism, then, offers a lot of upside potential. Ergo, it holds enormous potential for indigenous enterprise and indigenous entrepreneurs. American visitors spend more per head than visitors from Britain or mainland European countries. They also spend more on those value-added services which have the greatest multiplying effect on job creation here. Bord Failte have therefore rightly targeted this market for especial attention. This has already paid dividends – the increase in the number of North American visitors to Ireland has consistently beaten the growth for Europe generally, which means we are gaining in market share.

Joe Byrne, vice-president of Bord Failte for North America, is happy with their performance in the north-east of the US – in other words, the areas with the highest numbers of Irish-Americans. However, he is adamant that, to secure our long-term viability, we need to tap into the enormous non-Irish-American market.

"We are not, as yet, geared to cater for whatever extra demand might eventuate. Aeroplane seating and hotel beds are below what the market needs. Having persuaded the Americans that they should visit us, we have to route them through London. This effectively cuts overall numbers and, given London's diversions, shortens the stay of tourists who still insist on coming here; this, needless to say, negatively impinges on our revenues and on our jobs."

In the past, the compulsory Shannon stop over was a major disincentive to tourists wishing to visit Dublin. While that madness has, at last, been ended, we still lack sufficient direct capacity. Byrne believes that the decision by Aer Lingus to fly directly to Chicago rectified this anomaly somewhat.

Despite the fact that the Chicago link has increased total capacity by fourteen per cent, Byrne believes that there is still much room for improvement in this supposedly mature market. "We have to concentrate on getting a better regional spread from North America, as well as working on capacity. Compared to Britain and France we are over-performing in the numbers we get from the north-east of the US. But in areas like the south of the US and California we are under-performing."

Others agree with him. John Murray set up ETM Travel in 1987; each year his company brings about 3,000 Americans to Ireland for coach and golfing holidays. Murray believes that his customers have become more discerning from when he first started ten years ago. He therefore believes that if we wish to retain, let alone to build, on our market share, we must offer a higher value product. He believes we have to work on attracting Americans who do not have any ancestral connection with Ireland. "There is huge potential for job creation in tourism but we have to be more creative about how we attract them. We have people falling over themselves to go to London from the US outside the summer season. But we, on the other hand, seem to go in fads and end up with too many leisure centres or golf courses without the necessary backup."

Murray cites the example of building three golf courses in Wicklow, without having the required number of hotel beds in the area to cater for the numbers interested in going there. He cites accommodation problems in Dublin, Killarney and Galway, where nearly all of the hotel beds in those towns are booked out by March for the year. Although Murray believes the accommodation problem is being sorted out by market forces, he insists that the capacity problem has to be solved by giving more airlines direct access to Ireland.

Brian Moore, who founded Brian Moore International Travel twenty-three years ago, agrees with much of Murray's analysis. Moore's business, which is the second largest tour operator from the US, brings 15,000 Americans to Ireland on a range of holiday packages. He maintains that, although the tourist potential from North America remains enormous, it needs to be better cultivated. Recent increases in numbers have to be consolidated and, echoing Murray and Byrne, he too points to our lack of capacity. "There is no point having all of these marketing plans if the capacity is not there to take the American tourists across the Atlantic. Bums on seats and punters in hotel rooms are what really counts. We've got the punters. Give us the capacity and we'll do the rest."

For example he sells 16-day trips from New York which involves travelling first-class on Aer Lingus, staying in three five-star hotels and returning by cruise ship from Cork back to New York. The holiday costs $6,850. Although Moore knows that he can easily fill the vacancies and thereby illustrate the demand for top-quality, premium tourist projects to Ireland, he laments that we have only a handful of five-star hotels outside of Dublin. Until this capacity is increased, Moore cannot see the point in increasing marketing or other ultimately costly expenditures. Meanwhile, because of the efforts of people like Byrne, Moore and Murray, our tourist numbers are witnessing unprecedented growth. There has been a flourish of new businesses in Ireland, Dublin in particular. We have all seen the fleet of open-top buses run by Dublin Bus, providing historical and cultural tours of the city. But one individual who spotted the need for historical tours early on was Tommy Graham, a history graduate of Trinity College.

Twelve years ago, while an undergraduate Graham saw an opportunity to provide historical walking tours of Dublin. "At the time there were some others doing it, but I felt I could give a better service. The first year I did it, I was on my own, but when I found that it had gone down well, I got others involved in subsequent years." Graham recognised the need to provide an informative tour, which he says, told things as they were and didn't "treat people like idiots".

He quickly ran into difficulties when he found he couldn't put his leaflets into Bord Failte tourist offices, because he and his colleagues, although they were history graduates, had not taken an £800 certificate course. After some negotiation, they did sit the test and were then allowed to use Bord Failte offices for their promotional literature. "This gave us an additional boost and we found that it helped us to get more business. But how can small, struggling graduates be expected to give these tours when they can't afford to buy this over-priced badge?"

Typically, Graham's historical walking tours attract English speakers with some interest in finding out more about the country and the history of the city. "Since the IRA ceasefire in 1994 we have seen a dramatic increase in the number of English tourists to the city and their response to the tour is good and it goes down well with them."

Graham sees more potential for this type of business in Dublin and in other cities around the country. He never considered seriously expanding the business because he and his associates had other projects to occupy them: Graham himself is currently completing a PhD in history. "It's a bit like establishing a brand and we have done that over the years. We have actually had people coming back in subsequent years. I was a little concerned that my jokes on the tour hadn't changed."

Although there is now a wide range of walking tours available in Dublin, Graham believes the whole area of walking tours still remains under-developed, and with the growing tourist numbers in Dublin, there is clearly still a growing demand for these kinds of services which allow small operators like himself to compete with bigger concerns. Graham's other recent business venture is the production of *History Ireland*, a quarterly publication, which won an AIB Better Ireland Award. "*History Ireland* presents articles about Irish history in a readable and accessible way. We started it in Belfast through the Institute of Irish Studies. The fact is that there are not many publishing options for young historians and we have proved that there is a market for what they produce."

The magazine is already available in newsagents and bookshops throughout Ireland. Graham is trying to get a distribution deal for the magazine in Britain. The first issue came out in March 1993 and the issue now has a print run of over 10,000 copies, which is being sold to subscribers in Ireland, Britain and the US. Graham is toying with the idea of promoting the project on the Internet. "We are pleased with the way this publication has gone and we are looking at other options like educational publications. Although I am no longer as interested in history tours there is clearly, as my own experiences, the experiences of those who have copied me and the example of CIE's Dublin Bus tours all make evident, great potential for future generations of history graduates in providing these services."

Our tourist industry, then, is replete with opportunities for both big and small entrepreneurs alike. St Patrick's Day, Bloomsday and a host of other festivals which were under-marketed in the past, are all helping to keep tourist earnings as buoyant as our other major export earner: food.

CHAPTER FIVE

Feeding the World

The food and drink industry is arguably our premier national industry. Output from our food and agri-business companies exceeds £9 billion per annum; almost half of this is exported. The food industry accounts for twenty-nine per cent of GNP; for thirty-seven per cent of total manufacturing output in the Irish economy; twenty per cent of total exports and ten per cent of imports; it generates a positive annual trade balance in the order of £2 billion; £80 million worth of transport and haulage, £100 million worth of packaging and other services and between sixty-one per cent and ninety-four per cent of our national trade balance in recent years are directly dependent on it. It is, in short, our biggest and most vital national industry.

Three-quarters of employment in the industry is in indigenous, Irish-owned companies. It is directly responsible for twenty-two per cent of all manufacturing jobs and twenty-nine per cent of all jobs in Irish-owned industries. It accounts for thirty-seven per cent of all our output and twenty-two per cent of our employment. The industry is our single largest indigenous manufacturing employer, accounting for thirty per cent of all employment in Irish-owned industry. Furthermore, the import content of the food sector is much lower than any other part of Irish manufacturing industry, underlining, once again, the importance of a suitably reformed food industry in guaranteeing our future well-being.

Although our economy relies heavily on agriculture and its associated industries, our GDP per head is one of the EU's lowest, signalling, *inter alia*, the relatively low value-added content that our agricultural sector begets. However this is now a primary focus for the industry and it is improving. The potential for increased efficiency and increased profits is obvious.

Because the basic constituents of Irish agricultural output have changed so little over time, the grass base that has underpinned Irish agriculture since pre-Christian times will continue to underwrite our successes in the future. It is, however, unlikely, that the next decade will witness a recurrence of our recent phenomenal growth when Ireland's yield of common wheat per 100 kg/ha increased from 39.1 in 1973 to 82.1 in 1990. In other words, Ireland will remain competitive in this industry. Some land will move in and out of grain, depending on relative price relationships, but it looks as if the phenomenal transformation that has recently taken place in Irish grain, especially winter wheat, will not be repeated over the coming decades. The era of rapid growth is over.

Although we do not enjoy the economies of size of our competitors, many of our companies are flourishing. A number of key Irish food companies, private co-operatives and plcs, are now mini multi-nationals themselves. Twenty-five years ago, the idea of us having a number of companies with turnover in excess of £1 billion seemed outlandish. Now it is a happy reality.

A small Irish entrepreneurial coterie in this field now straddle the world. On present rates of growth, there may soon be Irish organisations with Irish-owned sophisticated production and distribution facilities for our core dairy and meat products right across Europe and beyond. The Kerry Group, one of the more prominent of this elite, is discussed at some length in our case study section.

With large exports, the Irish food industry could be said to be a global player. But while we have tended to develop our business around local strengths and weaknesses and to focus on issues such as pay-back to producers and employment, our competitors are locating capacity geographically according to least cost considerations. Major Irish food concerns, coming from a much narrower logistical base, run the risk of being strategically positioned out of our traditional markets. That is why we later compare ourselves, in some detail, to our British competitors.

The other sector experiencing increased globalisation is retailing. The Irish retailing sector now includes two major British multiples, Sainsbury's and Tesco which each have annual turnovers in excess of £10 billion. Collectively, these two are four times larger than the entire

Irish retail sector. The economies of scale of these two conglomerates dictates that they must source their products in Britain, as well as in Ireland. This has consequences for those Irish concerns which previously supplied Quinnsworth, Stewarts and Crazy Prices, all of which were recently purchased by Tesco. Clearly then, as our case-study comparison with our British competitors exemplifies, there are risks on more than one front with which the entire Irish food industry must contend.

Although comparisons with Britain clearly show why we should not be complacent, we should also realise that Irish companies are successfully meeting the challenges we discuss. Avonmore Waterford Group, Kerry, Kepak, Golden Vale and Irish Food Processors are trading with considerable success in Britain. These companies, though acting locally, are thinking globally and are determined to further cut costs and boost sales.

The sector's many difficulties, therefore, should not blind us to the very real opportunities which exist. Opportunities to supply the world's largest international companies with either prepared food ingredients which are then further processed by the brand-leader itself or to supply fully-prepared products which are then sold to consumers under the brand-leader's name.

However, competition between brand-leaders, between new entrants and between the chain stores' own copy-cat brands is intense. Given that the profitability of Irish-owned food companies is currently less than five per cent and that this slim margin is already coming under even more intense pressure, a long-term, viable and credible operational plan is needed. Although Kerry and Waterford, amongst others, are focusing on these areas, it is not at all clear that they or other Irish companies can thrive in this competitive environment.

David Dilger, chief executive of Greencore, stresses the need for conservative tactics and commitment to survival. He believes that companies should not attempt to expand abroad unless they first have secured a solid domestic base. Competing on familiar home turf is far easier than is playing in the cut-throat international arena.

Greencore's Erin Foods brand, which has a long-established reputation in Irish supermarkets, in particular in soups, casseroles and other mixes, highlights many of the issues within the industry. Until 1991, its distribution agency for Heinz comprised one-third of its business. That was until Heinz decided to enter the market itself. Overnight, the fortunes of Erin and Greencore were reversed. This forced Erin to look abroad. Erin targeted Sun Nutrition, the makers of Slimfast Products, who were looking for a European partner. Having won the business, it also targeted the private label sector for the British multiples. But there was a steep learning curve before Erin was successful. Ireland's distance and lack of accessibility proved major obstacles to cracking key British markets. Greencore have managed to overcome these obstacles with time, persistence and commitment.

Erin's strategy to expand its private label business consists of it analysing the own-brand products in a given multiple and zeroing in on what it thinks are the weakest products. Then Erin tries to develop a superior product to exploit the market gap, approaches the multiple and pitches for the business. While this may seem like Erin is scratching around for the crumbs, Dilger has said in the past on the issue that "if you pick up the crumbs for long enough, then one day you'll be sitting at the rich person's table".

Nationally, however, we will have to aim for more than the crumbs from the rich person's table. Otherwise, we may have to content ourselves with the leavings of others. Heinz, Nestlé and the other international food-producing giants are not the only threat. There are others. The recent arrival in Ireland of Tesco, Sainsbury's and Boots confirms that the European experience of food centralisation is being replicated in Ireland. In the top three dozen food categories, the top supplier has, on average, thirty-five per cent of market-share; the top three suppliers have sixty-five per cent. On average, two of the three top leaders in each of these national categories is also a well-known multi-national. A small number of Irish companies, if properly backed by the government, have the capacity to join this elite group. Clearly, opportunities exist to boost our capabilities in these areas.

Food ingredients, as noted earlier, and as stressed in our Kerry Foods case study, have also been targeted as an important market to enter. Although profit margins at five per cent to ten per cent are much higher than the two per cent to five per cent of the Irish dairy sector, this is a capital and technology-intensive industry. The industry's investment needs are about fifty per cent of annual sales. In our case study section, Kerry's Denis Brosnan explains what his company is are trying to do in this respect. Similarly, our Rye Valley case study shows how Irish companies can succeed in other lucrative niche markets. These, and our other case studies, are templates which must be copied, especially as there are many other niche markets waiting to be filled.

CASE STUDY – COOLEY DISTILLERIES

An old joke has it that Irish monks taught the Scots how to make whiskey over 1500 years ago and that the Scots are still learning. Perhaps the Scots could now return the favour and teach us how to market ours.

One hundred years ago Irish whiskey supplied sixty per cent of the world whiskey market. By 1970, our share had shrunk to a disgraceful one per cent. This clearly indicates our monumental failures in an industry which could so easily have brought much greater economic returns than it has. Because world-wide spirits' sales remain buoyant, Irish whiskey should be performing well. Indeed annually over 300,000 cases of Irish whiskey are sold in the US: when the 300,000 barrier was reached in 1995 it was the first time this level had been exceeded since 1915.

Because the drinks industry in Ireland, distilling and brewing in particular, is predominantly controlled by overseas corporations, most of these cases were produced by foreign-owned concerns. Cooley Distillers near Dundalk is, in fact, our only independent, Irish-owned whiskey company with three premium brands on offer. We now look at how Cooley, has performed in an area that is so pre-eminently Irish.

Dr John Teeling explains that the idea for the project came in 1970 when he was researching his PhD at Harvard University on the marketing of Irish whiskey in the US. Concomitantly, Willie McCarter, who formally ran the massive Fruit of the Loom business in Derry and Donegal, was also researching a whiskey thesis in MIT. When Teeling returned to Ireland and began the project, McCarter simultaneously bought out the old Watt business in Donegal. This later spawned Cooley's

Tyrconnel brand named after the flagship brand of one of Ulster's oldest distilleries.

Locke's is Cooley's flagship brand. It is a high-percentage malt-blended whiskey with a powerful maltiness and mellow sweetness and has been well-received by whiskey drinkers. The Tyrconnel, on the other hand, is a single-malt whiskey with an international flavour. It is now sold in fifteen countries as far apart as New Zealand and the US. With a fresh, malty bouquet, smooth sweet taste and delicate dry finish, the Tyrconnel has been well-received. The horse on the label is a special commemorative label the Watt family designed for the bottle after they entered a horse named The Tyrconnel in the Irish Classic, the Queen Victoria Plate, in 1876. The horse won at odds of 100-1.

Kilbeggan whiskey, produced in the town of Kilbeggan, first appeared as a John Locke brand over a hundred years ago. The brand was sold successfully until Locke's ceased production in the 1950s. Cooley's has brought the whiskey back into production and has successfully launched Kilbeggan into the international market to complement the success of the Tyrconnel.

Cooley, although producing high-quality products, has its own problems which clearly exemplify the difficulties inherent in tackling the international whiskey barons. A considerable portion of the finance, which allowed Dr John Teeling, the former UCD academic turned entrepreneur, to set up the Cooley business, came from BES funds. The structure of the Cooley Group of companies is such that the Cooley company does not manufacture whiskey, but instead buys it from a number of BES-funded companies which are responsible for distilling and storing the range of products.

But Cooley has had other problems. The Pernod-Ricard-owned Irish Distillers Group's made a £22 million take-over bid for the company in 1993 which, if successful, would have shut down the distillery and sold off the Cooley whiskey stocks into international markets. While IDG waited for approval for its take-over plan, it agreed to buy some £700,000 worth of Cooley's whiskey stocks in order to keep Cooley solvent. Dr Teeling insisted that Cooley have an option to buy these stocks back at a later stage. The Competition Authority, however, turned down the take-over, in the public interest and Cooley was made to buy back the

£700,000 worth of whiskey causing further difficulties.

The Government's heavy-handed manner towards Cooley exemplifies the problems the lack of a secondary market causes in Irish business causes. If the Competition Authority hadn't intervened, Cooley would by now have probably been totally run-down and amalgamated into a larger concern.

The company faced a number of financial crises in the years following the unsuccessful take-over by IDG. The fact that Dr Teeling and the others who founded the company, wanted to sell it to IDG, has made it more difficult for them to carry the company forward following the Competition's Authority's recommendations. The whiskey market in Ireland tends to be very brand-loyal and brand-specific, which basically means that punters will almost always specify the particular brand they want. This makes it very difficult for new brands to crack the Irish or British markets.

Cooley has, as a result, enjoyed only limited success in its home market. Although it is selling comparatively well in Britain and other European countries, its most notable successes have been in Germany and the US. Cooley has been innovative in its attempts to break into new markets. For example, it has developed contracts with a number of own-label brands with British and Irish multiple foodstore chains including Sainsbury's in Britain and Quinnsworth's in Ireland. Again this was seen as a tactical ploy to avoid directly competing with the giant IDG.

Despite the best efforts of the management, the company still faces financial difficulties. Should it eventually liquidate, there will be a certain irony for any prospective entrants into the whiskey market in Ireland. If the IDG bid had been allowed to go ahead, it would have proved to be reasonably lucrative for the investors and backers of Cooley. It would also have provided a ready-made market and value for shares in Cooley, even though the operation would have been closed down immediately. A successful buy-out from IDG could have provided an incentive for a budding entrepreneur to set up a rival distillery, in the hope of emulating Cooley and eventually selling out to IDG for a profit. With the Competition Authority's refusal to allow the acquisition, if Cooley liquidates, we are not likely to see anyone else try to do the same thing again for some time. Irish whiskey will remain lock, stock and barrel in foreign hands.

Dr Teeling is not entirely pessimistic. He maintains that, though the company will continue to lose money for another few years, it will eventually prove profitable. Cooley's future problems are analogous to those of other businesses in the food and beverages industry. "Our weakness is the lack of a domestic market. The case of Irish whiskey which had such a strong position a hundred years ago highlights the problems. The industry here failed to respond to consumer tastes and changes."

Cooley's also exemplifies distilling's many specific problems. Distilling demands large up-front cash injections. Cash-flow is delayed until maturity which, though being a bare minimum of three years, is more typically between seven and ten years in duration. Because this delayed and staggered return on the up-front investment significantly increases its risk profile. Teeling maintains that: "Cooley will make money but it will not make enough money to cover the amount of risk that has been involved and the stress attached to it."

For Dr Teeling, the Cooley project was based on an ultimately flawed financial model which he developed. "I had been involved in so many businesses before Cooley but I had never built anything up from scratch and I think that was a factor." The company employs fifty people on a part-time basis. Despite the risks, they have lost only two staff members over the last few years – evidence as much of the lack of opportunity on the Cooley peninsula as on the long-term viability of the company. This sense of stagnancy highlights some of the long-term obstacles confronting our drinks industry as well as the potential this sector has for growth.

There are more fundamental problems which we cannot avoid. The tiny size of our domestic market and our lack of a manufacturing or entrepreneurial tradition, all impinge on our potential for sustained success. "I have gone to a lot of places, places like South Africa, where I have tried to sell Irish whiskey. It is very difficult and logistical problems are such that my market for selling whiskey is thousands of miles away."

He points to the high cost of stationing sales teams in far-flung countries which our small, albeit growing food and drink companies find difficult to sustain. In this regard, Dr Teeling believes the work being carried out by An Bord Bia is most beneficial. The Food Board provides over seventy-five per cent of the cost of travelling to a food show or exhibition to sell a product. Similarly, it bears some of the marketing costs.

However, Ireland's geographical remoteness from the major markets for spirits presents its own logistical problems. Dr Teeling explains that it is therefore a lengthy, costly and time-consuming process to introduce a new product to these markets. He believes that the only real long-term sustainable industries for Ireland will come through agriculture, tourism and culture. "These are the only areas which will yield added value. I don't see a future for manufacturing in Ireland. We are not a manufacturing country and we do not have any comparative advantage in manufacturing."

Dr Teeling cannot see our software and high-tech successes continuing to grow, untroubled, into the future. "That is not to say that IDA Ireland or whoever should not be out there attracting these companies, because they have done a wonderful job." He believes that, now that we realise that jobs from foreign-owned companies cannot solve our unemployment problem, substantial progress can be made. "This realisation has led to a focus on entrepreneurship which is healthy, but it must be realised that entrepreneurship, if it were hugely successful, will not solve Ireland's economic problems either."

Dr Teeling believes that we must therefore develop our three core areas: food – because it is based on raw materials which we have in abundance – tourism and culture, because we can market Ireland as a brand name. He also sees the obstacles developing these three sectors will present. To illustrate these he highlights Dublin's recent tourist boom. Each weekend 3,000 people from Britain come to Dublin to eat, drink and be merry. Ireland, Dublin in particular, has become a fashionable place in which to chill out. We should, he believes, harness and convert into hard cash that demand.

If the attraction is the Irish pub phenomenon, then that should be marketed and exported. Dr Teeling laments that others have beaten us to the job of marketing ourselves to the world. One of the most successful Irish pub companies in Europe is owned by Guinness, the British-quoted multi-national. The biggest Irish bar in Europe, which has three floors, two of which have Irish music playing seven nights per week, is 'Irish Rover' in Madrid. This pub, which is jam-packed round the clock with affluent, young Spaniards, is managed by Spaniards and owned by the Dutch Heineken conglomerate. A few Cooley whiskey bottles aside, this Irish concept has only limited Irish involvement.

When asked why entrepreneurs have been so thin on the ground in Ireland over the decades, Dr Teeling maintains that, though social obstacles such as begrudgery are still prevalent, albeit not as much as they were in the past, we must probe deeper into our collective psyche if we wish to find the answers. "Things have changed a lot in the last twenty-five years and I believe begrudgery is not the force it used to be."

He believes that job security and cushioned respectability remain central to our collective psyche. Whilst explaining how well-documented is the tendency amongst our school-leavers to want to secure permanent and pensionable jobs in the bank or to become school teachers themselves, he maintains that we have progressed from his days as a lecturer of first-year commerce students in UCD where fifteen out of a class of 300 would want to go into business. "Studies have indicated that 0.5 per cent of the population are entrepreneurial. Colleges don't produce them, although they contribute to the process. But if we look at who is emigrating, there could be an argument for showing that we are losing most of the best potential entrepreneurs."

Dr Teeling maintains that agencies like An Bord Bia and Forbairt do a good job, but that, ultimately they face a mammoth, if not impossible task. If Ireland requires 40,000 jobs every year to off-set job losses, and if we accept that most small firms will never hire more than five employees, Ireland would need 8,000 new start-ups per year just to keep our dole queues at their current levels.

Several obstacles, he maintains, militate against an entrepreneurial upsurge here. He particularly cites the issue of access to risk capital. He criticises Irish banks for not taking risks although, he interestingly declares, it is not really their job to take them. "Risks are going to be taken by others and we do need greater venture capital. I don't like dealing with Irish banks. When you go to Irish banks with an idea which is different, you are likely to come out badly, because they are not going to take the necessary risks. They tend not to lend to entrepreneurs and I don't think they have a significant role to play in financing start-up business."

Dr Teeling believes a State-run, Small Business Administration, similar to the one in the US, which gives out small loans to new businesses, is long overdue here. "The Business Expansion Scheme has helped to provide some of that risk finance. But the scheme worked well until the lawyers got their hands on it and it has now become completely bogged down in regulations. The problem is that they now want it to be risk-free and that is not what is required."

CASE STUDY – GEOFF READ AND BALLYGOWAN WATER

While Irish whiskey production is dominated by Irish Distillers Group, one area of the beverage industry, which has recently produced a bevy of budding entrepreneurs, is bottled water. Although exports of bottled water exceed domestic consumption, it will be a long and hard process to achieve significant growth due to its low value to volume ratio. That said, the industry has come a long way since Geoff Read more or less invented the Irish bottled water industry in 1979.

Indeed, if we agree that Ireland must build on what she has, Geoff Read, Ballygowan Water's founder, has done just that. He has, in the Ballygowan product, successfully marketed a modern-day version of Ireland. Although this falls short of Tony O'Reilly's vision of us selling Ireland as a quality brand, it represents a giant step forward in the right direction.

A hangover inspired his success. Recovering from a Friday-night party in London, he decided to buy a bottle of mineral water in a local Underwood's store. He bought a bottle of French mineral water but not before noticing that the shop had a large range of mineral waters on sale. Sipping the purchase throughout the day convinced him that he could make a product superior not only to the brand he had bought but to the other ones Underwood's were selling as well.

Geoff Read founded Ballygowan at a time when our consumption of bottled water was minimal and, more importantly, when the notion of buying water to drink on its own was an anathema to most of us. But the major world players in bottled water, Perrier and Evian, were already selling their products here, albeit in comparatively small quantities. However, attitudes were changing. Because consumers were becoming more health conscious, there was a growing demand for environmentally-friendly, non-fattening products such as Ballygowan. Geoff Read worked hard to satiate what developed into an apparently insatiable demand.

Following both the domestic and international successes of Ballygowan, a small, 'cottage bottled-water industry' has mushroomed with no less than twenty brands of Irish spring water being currently available. Geoff Read believes that the Irish market has reached saturation point and that many of the existing small players are not likely to be around in a decade's time. As a result, Ballygowan, by the far the largest operator in this industry in Ireland, faces a range of questions about its future. Although the brand is internationally successful, Ballygowan must ask how it can continue to grow and compete with such international giants as Evian and Perrier, both of which are ultimately controlled by two of the largest food companies in the world.

This stark marketing reality was one of the factors which ultimately forced Read to sell the company to Cantrell and Cochrane, which is owned by the international drinks giant, Grand Metropolitan. Although naturally pleased with his own considerable success, he doubts that other existing Irish mineral-water companies can reach the same level of international success as Ballygowan, which is now the brand leader in both Britain and Ireland.

His scepticism derives from the all-important ownership and distribution questions. "Most of the major food and drink companies operating in Ireland are internationally owned. Ownership of successful companies is a major issue which has to be looked at. I believe there is a need for a strategic plan for Irish food and drink companies, which will take a realistic look at these issues and how these companies can compete internationally."

Read highlights the brands of Bailey's and Ballygowan, which have shown that organic non-polluted products can achieve success on the global market. He suggests that issues, like finding niche markets for organically-produced goods and similar products, could be promoted in conjunction with Bord Failte. "If we look at the image that we present of ourselves internationally, and that is the job of Bord Failte, these things can be done in tandem." Other State agencies such as An Bord Bia and Forbairt could, he believes, provide more back-up to growing Irish food and drink companies, in terms of providing non-financial support and personnel.

He agrees with Greencore's David Dilger that we should look for niche markets which the bigger players have neglected. The sheer scale and size of the major world players in food and drink prevents us from doing that. "One of the keys to the success of Ballygowan was that it was valued on the basis of things like its packaging and its origins, namely the presentation of Ireland as clean and an environmentally-pure country."

He is quick to point out that Ballygowan is not the cheapest product on the shelves and is never likely to be. But, by introducing a premium on the product, by selling it to specific markets and by achieving product differentiation through packaging and marketing, it succeeded where others failed. "We developed Ballygowan at a time when foreign brands were preferred over Irish brands. We have reversed that trend by developing a superior product packaged in a superior way."

That said, there are obstacles galore to other start-up or fast-growth firms replicating Ballygowan's performance. Read believes there is not enough room in the Irish spring-water market for all of the existing players. "This also comes down to one of the reasons I sold the business. The sector has changed and become more commoditised. There is no effective regulation, and for many of the operators it is not the key part of their business."

There is probably only really room for a maximum of three bottled-water players in Ireland. "The domestic market will not sustain a whole load of Irish spring-water companies. I had built up Ballygowan to become the largest company of its kind in these islands, but the consumption rates in Ireland are still comparatively small. With Irish people only consuming eight or nine litres of bottled water per person, per year, the economies are stacked against some of our smaller players."

Because of its high brand identification and its attention both to quality and detail, he sees a great international potential in the Ballygowan product. When, as is inevitable, some of these other manufacturers fail, Read believes that greater import penetration will occur. Ireland has always supported international products quite well, and there is likely to be a wider diversity of products available. But despite this pessimistic outlook for Irish manufacturers, Read still plans to go into business again in a related area: "I still believe there are lots of opportunities for new companies in the food and drink industry. Other entrepreneurs continue to develop new products which can achieve international status, and that sort of thing is happening all of the time."

Real reward, he believes, comes from maintaining liquidity. Read points out that the successful business-people working in a quoted plc have all of the benefits of salary, pension contributions, performance bonuses and share options, whereas entrepreneurs are involved in a higher-risk venture and do not achieve the same liquidity until they decide to sell the business on. "The only measure of success is financial gain and profit. There is a need to encourage people to build up businesses and sell them on and respect that there is nothing wrong with that. It is nearly impossible to build up a big business in Ireland."

Ballygowan could not have achieved what it did without the removal of one tax obstacle shortly after the company was set up. Bottled water was subject to a table water duty of 37.2 per cent and VAT of twenty-one per cent. This effectively doubled the price of the water on the shelf, and meant he could not compete with the imported products. The abolition of the VAT on bottled water provided the vital boost to sales which ultimately allowed the company to blossom.

Read sees a lot of current EU legislation presenting further obstacles to entrepreneurial activity. He cites, in particular, the EU's social equity legislation and, whilst stating that everyone is entitled to a decent wage, he feels that the thinness of Ireland's markets ensures that these legislative changes will tip many otherwise vibrant Irish firms into bankruptcy and liquidation. He believes that, given Ireland's demographic and critical mass short-comings, these reforms should be wavered in our case. "If you create something which is totally original, because of the small population, it is nearly impossible to sustain a manufacturing facility which is up to necessary standards. Big players can dump products on the Irish market so easily. Scale is a big issue in anything you want to manufacture."

All of these factors add to the risk the entrepreneur takes in setting up a business in Ireland. It then becomes important for the State agencies and banks in particular to share part of that risk. Read believes our banks are risk-averse and that, as a consequence, they don't provide anything like the level of venture capital that is required to bring new enterprises forward at a socially satisfying rate. "Their security requirements are too high. Many of our prospective investors are not prepared to take risks. In one way the Business Expansion Schemes were useful for getting risk capital, but the operation of the scheme needed to be more defined and given some focus."

BES schemes ended up as little more than a tax dodge. He is extremely critical of the amount of money that is invested, through BES funds, in hotels and restaurants, in particular. "These are not the kinds of business which we should be focusing on with one of the few forms of risk capital available. The focus should be on businesses which are going to create long-term quality jobs, which go towards building up an industry."

Ballygowan benefited enormously from its involvement with Mercury, the British venture capital fund, which Read says has played a major role in the success of a number of Irish companies. "Where are the Irish banks? I went to Mercury with Ballygowan because I knew I would get a more positive response. With Ballygowan, Bank of Ireland were our bankers and I cannot fault them in the services they provided, and the fact that they were with us all the way. But there has to be someone there providing the necessary risk capital. I think Irish banks just don't see it as their role."

Although Read observes other serious obstacles to entrepreneurial endeavour in our social structure, he is quick to knock the idea that begrudgery is the principal cultural obstacle to the development of enterprise here. For Read, begrudgery is rolled out all too often as an excuse for our many other anti-entrepreneurial short-comings. "I see the period from the time you leave school to when you get married, as the key period for any prospective entrepreneur. It is during this period that you can most afford to take risks. Most people are restricted from taking these risks because they get married or they are in college."

The entrepreneurial character is, therefore, crystallised between leaving school and getting married, but that because of the closeness of the family unit and its importance in Irish society, this crystallisation often does not materialise. "There is a perception that you need a degree or at least to go to college for four years. There needs to be more emphasis in school that being in business is an appropriate thing to do and that it is just as valid as being a doctor or a solicitor. If you ask people in school what they want to do, nobody ever claims to want to be an entrepreneur or a manufacturer."

He follows this up by adding that in school there should also be a greater focus on business skills, where students can learn negotiating skills, which would enable them to leave school, "without thinking their whole being is about passing exams". Read, though an electronics graduate is, one could say, almost roguishly proud when he says that he never really used his electronics expertise, but that his college experiences selling leather jackets to his college buddies probably stood him in better stead in later life.

Although much fruitful time could be spent trying to identify the gestation of the entrepreneurial gene in Geoff Read, there are more pressing matters the successful entrepreneur must address. Bearing in mind the fact that the food and drink industries are dominated by a handful of global businesses, Read maintains that eventually selling the company, as he did with Ballygowan, is an important part of the process. "There comes a time when you are no longer able to build up the business on your own and you are just involved in the day-to-day drudge of management. It is a feature of any entrepreneur to feel they are operating in a dynamic environment. They tend to be insecure and they want the reward and the recognition of the value of the business – something which they have built up. There is also a need to secure your position, in case it all starts to go wrong."

After selling Ballygowan, Read stayed on at the group's London office, sourcing new markets and handling exports. But he eventually decided to leave the group altogether because, as he says, it was difficult to fit in after it had been acquired. "The management of large companies tend to employ people whom they don't see as a threat. The entrepreneur, more often than not, does not fit into the corporate model. This fact, that the entrepreneur likes building and growing things, needs to be recognised earlier in the system."

CASE STUDY – CAN WE COMPETE IN FOOD?

Britain's importance as a major market for our food and drinks sector is paramount. It absorbs forty per cent of products from this sector. Its population of fifty-seven million, compared to a relatively restrictive 3.5 million here, means that our upside potential, especially given our common tastes and packaging histories, is significantly greater in Britain than in Ireland.

Potential rewards bring potential risks. Britain, which is by far our most important market for "processed, added-value food products" which have been the target of recent expansionary plans, has the potential to bring all of our plans to nought.

The threat comes from the ability of British brand manufacturers to supplant our own brands on both the domestic and international markets. The increasing presence of British retailers on this island must also be taken into account. Sainsbury's, Tesco, Marks and Spencers, Boots and the many other retailers setting up here have the capacity to squeeze out our home-grown distributors from the major towns and cities. Although Dunnes Stores have been drawing attention to the sourcing policies of their competitors, the Irish trade union movement has also drawn attention to the consequences for their members of sourcing food and other material from outside of Ireland.

We should be in no doubt about where this will lead. If current uncompetitiveness is not addressed, this will eventually relegate the twenty-six counties to a provincial offshoot of the British market. Jobs that currently exist in the Irish manufacturing, distribution and retail market are being replaced by a central warehousing system for British-produced grocery goods and manufacturing will, as a consequence, be increasingly relocated to sites in Britain.

Although the food and drink sector has been targeted for long-term strategic development in a succession of official reports, typical of which were the Food Industry Task Force, the Culliton Report and the Moriarty Report, even a cursory comparison of our industry with that of Britain, highlights a galaxy of problems. Unless addressed as a matter of extreme urgency, these obstacles to growth threaten to undermine medium-term development strategies for the food and drink industry. Indeed, given Britain's key role as a major market and as the source of fifty per cent of our total food imports, employment and output in the Irish food industry will be crucially and, perhaps, even ultimately, affected by our competitiveness vis à vis Britain.

The competitiveness of the Irish food and drink sector is further seriously undermined by our relatively high manufacturing costs. The average industrial hourly rate of earnings in Britain, if we omit the overpriced London area, is fourteen per cent lower than here. PRSI and other hidden taxes inflate Irish industrial costs even more. Natural gas is 122 per cent more expensive and telecommunications and insurance costs are much higher here than they are in Britain.

Worse still perhaps, there is often little correlation between government policy and market reality. In the dairy industry, for example, cheese production continues to fall and production of butter and skimmed milk powder is on the increase. This is totally contrary to stated policy. Nor is this state of affairs confined to the dairy industry. Vacuum-packed beef markets in Britain have been lost. In both the dairy and beef industries, there is a worrying shift away from the commercial market in Britain towards subsidised support-driven outlets mainly outside of the EU. Added to this is the fact that Irish beef companies are being forced to heavily invest in British-based production plants.

The uncompetitive situation outlined above with regard to raw material prices and manufacturing costs is making the Irish food industry more dependent on subsidies and supports than before. While this dependence on subsidised outlets would leave the sector strategically vulnerable at any time, it is particularly dangerous for the food sector when these subsidised outlets have been specially targeted for reduction under CAP reform and the Uruguay Round.

Although the British market must be central in any strategy aimed at enhancing output and employment growth, in comparison to Britain, we are not competitive. Given common brand manufacturing, Britain represents a very real threat in terms of replacing output and employment in the Irish grocery sector if the current uncompetitive situation continues. A situation where the sector's ability to supply its major market is being eroded, and its own relatively tiny home-market base is being undermined, represents a fundamental threat to the survival of a vital national industry.

Our other cost disincentives must also, in the interests of national self-preservation, be addressed. Although the government cannot expect EMU to be costless, it must recognise that it will require significant reductions in the costs to Irish manufacturers across a range of areas such as taxes, labour costs and public utility prices. Government targets for the food industry in terms of job creation and increased sales are quite specific. But the means, by which these targets will be met, are much more difficult to comprehend. For example, although much of our economic future is being staked on EMU participation, the consequences of such participation, particularly if Britain abstains from membership, is not at all clear. If Ireland joins EMU and Britain abstains, it is entirely feasible that the Irish currency (the Euro) will once again appreciate against the British pound. Should such a scenario unfold, the cost of Irish goods in Britain would once again increase and Irish companies would once again lose out in the competitiveness battle. Rye Valley, our next case study, supplies the British market with ready-made meals and loses £100,000 per penny increase in the exchange rate with sterling.

Under EMU, should Britain abstain, employment in secondary processing, which is targeted to expand, will, most likely, contract as investment moves to the lower-cost base which pertains in Britain. Like any dynamic sector, the Irish food industry must be aware of EMU and similar economic processes. It cannot stand still or tread water. It must change, adapt and expand in order to survive. In particular, it must retain a competitive edge in order to attract highly mobile capital investment. In all such strategic thinking, comparison with Britain is crucial. Britain is also our major competitor for inward investment. Existing multi-nationals based in Ireland or those seeking a new presence in the EU will inevitably compare Britain and Ireland as potential locations for any new investment. Based on current competitiveness costs and currency rates, there is no economic basis for investing in Ireland rather than in Britain.

This argument is reinforced when we consider that our special EU status and accompanying structural fund grants are due to expire. When these cash injections cease, our true lack of competitiveness vis à vis Britain will be exposed. The consequences for food, our major industry, may well be quite traumatic. Starkly put, if we cannot compete with Britain, we cannot compete and we will face decline rather than growth.

However, despite this gloomy prognosis, our next few examples show how, despite the disadvantages they labour under, Irish firms can still compete against the British and other foreign sources of competition.

CASE STUDY – RYE VALLEY

Rye Valley, which is based in Carrickmacross, County Monaghan, is successfully exporting its products to Britain. It was set up in 1988 by four former Cork Marts/IMP employees. It manufactures ready-made meals for British supermarkets, employs 300 people and has an annual turnover of over £32 million. Rye Valley has been the kind of success story we need to repeat elsewhere.

As a result of the Rye Valley experience both Pat Doyle, Rye Valley's managing director and his partner, Pat O'Leary, praise the role Forbairt and An Bord Bia are playing in the Irish food industry. However, Doyle believes that FÁS should spend less of its budget training the unemployed and more providing additional training for people who are already working.

Doyle remains grateful to Larry Goodman, who took a forty per cent stake in the business when it was first set up. It proved useful to have a 'big brother' investor who was supportive without dominating the business. This 'big brother' helped the business to secure credibility in looking for additional finance and approaching customers. Goodman sold his stake in 1991 – thirty per cent was bought by ICC Bank, while the founders bought the other ten per cent. The early days though, were hard. At one stage, having left their jobs, the four struggling entrepreneurs were turned down for financial assistance from the IDA on three separate occasions: they were living off social welfare at the time.

Most of Rye Valley's products are marketed as own-label goods in the British multiples market; Rye Valley has avoided the branded market. Although this tactic saved them from directly competing with the major multi-nationals, Doyle now maintains that there are no longer any unprotected niche markets left in the food industry: the food giants are trying to increase, no matter how minutely, their own market-share. Coca-Cola, for example, now have it written into their mission statement that their aim is now not only to refresh the world, as they put it, but to increase market share as much as possible. Rye Valley face conglomerates who similarly want to increase their market share at the expense of minnows of smaller enterprises.

Rye Valley is, however, far from cowed by their opposition. As Doyle explains, "We are already competing against the big multi-national players. It does not mean the end of the smaller operator. Smaller firms, like us, can develop the ability to change to customers' tastes and needs, can get closer to the customer by face-to-face contact and can often be more innovative."

On this latter point, Doyle is bullish about the future of the Irish food industry and he believes that if some of our uncompetitive diseconomies were removed, Irish companies could have a sustainable future. Doyle notes that the pattern of sourcing raw materials outside Ireland is becoming more popular as is the temptation for food and packaging companies to develop their British operations at the expense of their Irish operations.

CASE STUDY – THE KERRY GROUP

The Kerry Group is one of our few major dairy-based companies which have broken out of the dead-end of milk. Kerry is one of our country's most successful businesses; it holds real global potential. Although it is involved in food production in three continents, in the last four years it has increasingly focused on the food-ingredients industry.

The company has world-wide group sales in excess of £1.3 billion and makes profits of £70 million annually. Over the next five years, Kerry expects the proportion of its total business – from ingredients – to increase even more significantly than it has in the last five years. In this regard it has continued on its expansion trail, recently acquiring the Franco-Italian Ciprial and the British Dalgety food ingredients businesses. Kerry has further plans to enter into other lucrative niche markets. It intends, for example, to increasingly service the large multinational food manufacturers in the branded convenience and prepared food sector.

Kerry had its beginnings as a Kerry-based dairy co-operative and, despite the international successes of the company, group chief executive, Denis Brosnan, says: "My advice will always be to keep the core block of shares in Kerry. We have worked thirty years to build it up."

Brosnan, the son of a local farmer, attended St Brendan's School in Killarney, before completing a Master's Degree in Food Science at University College Cork. Although his first job was as a detergent salesman, he soon joined Golden Vale as a production manager, and ran a factory for the company before moving to their London offices. He returned to his native county in 1972 as general manager of a new North Kerry Milk Producers' casein plant in Listowel. Two years later the Kerry Co-op was born as a response to the rationalisation plans for the dairy industry. Brosnan was the principal founding partner and raised £1 million from Kerry farmers to financially kick-start the enterprise.

During those early days of Kerry Co-op Creameries, Brosnan was outlining his plans for the group to a large gathering of Kerry farmers, and invited questions from the floor. One of the farmers asked, "And tell me how much are we paying you to do all this?" Brosnan replied, "I'm not going to tell you, but whatever it is, it is not half enough." The answer summed up Brosnan's tenacity, which has played such a crucial role in building up the Kerry empire. He hand-picked thirteen key staff in 1974, almost all of whom have remained with the company to this day.

Within three years, they had trebled Kerry's turnover to £60 million. Ten years later, in 1985, Brosnan masterminded the flotation of the business, and played a key role in transforming the group into a major operation employing 3,000 people in Ireland and 4,000 abroad. From the outset, he saw the need for diversification and by the late 1970s, the co-op had begun to reduce commodity production and increase its output of casein, a milk by-product used as a food ingredient. He charged the company's research and development division with finding more value-added products and acquisitions continued in Limerick, Cork and Galway.

Brosnan is well aware of the risks the changing international environment presents. The enormous competitive challenge which today's Irish food sector faces is unprecedented. He believes that how we strategically address these challenges will determine the future structure of our agri-food industry. Our response to these challenges is, he insists, a matter of the highest national importance and, given the centrality of agriculture to our economy, it will have profound economic effects on us all.

He believes that the Irish food industry is at the peak of a golden era. This 'golden era' has been, in large part, funded by the EU. "The food industry has been hugely successful here, but we cannot afford to sit on our laurels." He sees Eastern Europe presenting us with an enormous threat. "Once the politicians clasp the nettle of Eastern Europe, we will see big changes."

The food division of Kerry Foods has its headquarters in England. Brosnan notes that a number of leading Irish food companies, including Kerry, Avonmore-Waterford Group, Larry Goodman's Irish Food Processors and the Clonee-based Kepak, have all bought production facilities in Britain. He is also aware that British multiple-chain supermarkets have cracked the domestic Irish market and that they will produce where it is cheapest to do so. Brosnan believes that our companies selling in Britain will increasingly have to source their production facilities there as well.

Although Brosnan attributes this tendency to centralise to market forces, he is adamant that, even as Irish companies move off-shore, it is important that they be encouraged to keep their decision-making here. "You have to keep the key decision makers in Ireland. Because, when it comes to closing plants they will close the plants which are further from home and keep the one's which are closer."

Allied to this strategic concept, Brosnan further believes that we must move more quickly into value-added areas before the East European countries price us entirely out of the low-end of the market. He justifies Kerry's diversification strategies on the grounds that they do not want to be elbowed or priced out of the markets they have so assiduously built up over the years. "Certainly some products have to be made elsewhere. For example, we bought Ciprial, the French-based fruit business. That business sells forty per cent of its produce in Britain, and it must be produced in France where they have the necessary climate."

Although Ireland's comparative advantage has traditionally rested with milk and meat, Brosnan is adamant that we must develop beyond them. "We still produce a significant percentage of our milk on a seasonal basis. The milk advantage is not going to do that much for us in the long term. There is also an advantage in beef. But again, the beef herd often comes from the dairy herd and so there is a restriction because of seasonality."

Brosnan is not interested in merging with or taking over another Irish company. He maintains it would simply be enmeshing the group into a milk business which is both heavily regulated by the EU and which is very cyclical in nature and – more significantly – which is, perhaps, ultimately doomed.

Although he bemoans the relatively small size of our companies, when compared to the multi-nationals with whom we must compete, he does not see any real point in merging with any of the Avonmore-Waterfords. "I would have to ask is there any real benefit for Kerry in merging with one of the others. I would have to say no there is not. Then you have the question of whether it would benefit Ireland for any of the others to merge with each other. I believe that may well be an issue they will have to consider."

Kerry have, in fact, been busily diversifying out of milk. Today, over half of Kerry's income is derived from its food ingredients' sector; over two thirds of its turnover is now being generated in North America.

It first began expanding into food ingredients with the 1988 acquisition for £130 million of Beatreme Foods. Since then it has continued to strategically diversify out of its original Irish-based dairy business. Prior to its acquisition of DCA, it was already selling food ingredients into sixty countries; DCA added a significant British sector and also brought it new markets in Australasia. The group has plans for further expansion in South America and Asia.

Cautiously bullish about the future potential for Irish food companies, he sees the smaller size of Irish companies as presenting several opportunities. "Small food and ingredients companies can do things which the larger players cannot do. Their entrepreneurial spirit will continue to help the entire industry."

Brosnan praises the records of both Forbairt and An Bord Bia. "The key question for these agencies is to decide whether to put all their money in small entities or to give it to the big players. It is a fundamental decision which has to be made at the start, and we need to give both of these entities time to make a lasting impression. But I do think their overall approach has been right to date."

The Kerry Group started as a farmer's co-operative in 1972, and the co-operative held a 52.2 per cent majority stake in the group until quite recently. Though issues, including a hostile take-over bid, may have to be addressed in the future, Brosnan is prepared for such contingencies. He muses on the negative impact such a bid might have for the wider Kerry community. One of the possible downsides of such development could be the loss of the group's key role in promoting County Kerry for tourism. Executives from the Kerry Group, Brosnan prominent amongst them, have been centrally involved in promoting the interests of the entire Kerry community.

His own interests include horse-racing and golf. He is the chairman of the Irish Horse Racing Authority and of Leisure Holdings, a sports and hotel group which evolved from the bloodstock company, Leading Shires, and Swing, a venture which provides top golf facilities for tourists at our best-known courses. He was also chairman of Kerry Airport, where he oversaw an investment of over £6 million to upgrade to international status Kerry's regional airport at Farranfore.

Brosnan places his work with tourism in the context of why Kerry Co-op was set up in the first place. "The success of the Kerry Group as a whole has often overshadowed the fact that Kerry dairy farms are still small in size and would have difficulty surviving in a total free-market context. Sixty percent of farmers here have a quota of less than 20,000 gallons; this is three times the national average of twenty per cent. Similarly, eighty-two per cent of Kerry farmers have quotas of less than 30,000 gallons, compared to forty per cent nationally. From the outset, keeping County Kerry and her people economically viable has been problematic."

Because tourism has been an economic life-line to Kerry, Brosnan's involvement in promoting Farranfore Airport was as much motivated by wider, tourist-related concerns as it was by the needs of the Group. When Denis Brosnan was chairperson of Kerry Airport, he raised several million pounds from the community, private investors and the State. Farranfore now has trans-Atlantic chartered flights directly from the US. The airport also has numerous chartered flights from Germany and Switzerland.

"One of the difficulties is that budget tourists are now coming to the east of the country in greater numbers. This is partially fuelled by competition among the airlines on routes into Dublin. So large numbers are coming into Dublin, but tourism is achieving very little growth elsewhere."

He is nonetheless, proud of the contribution he and Kerry have made to developing the region. The airport is now profitable and Brosnan is redirecting his considerable energies into other projects. He is also involved in Kerry Holidays, which is a specialist holiday company based in Tralee. Brosnan explains Kerry's considerable altruistic involvement in these projects as part of the much wider social agenda already discussed. "We have not made any money out of these projects but we have tried to act as a catalyst in promoting the whole region. You have to remember that the county only has a population of 100,000 people."

County Kerry has been fortunate in having a major corporate entity based in the area. The Kerry Group directly employs 1,500 people in County Kerry and Brosnan accepts that other counties have been historically less fortunate than the Kingdom. "It is much more difficult when you do not have a major enterprise backing you up." He cites how the company is perceived as a guarantor for Kerry Airport by lending its support to it in such an upfront way. "Kerry is an exceptional county which has a community spirit and has also produced probably more business-people than any other county in Ireland," he controversially alleges.

Returning to the many problems our tourism industry has in realising its full potential, he says: "It is only when we all realise that we must have sufficient seats at the right prices on planes, that we will see the required numbers coming here. We need competitively-priced seats to get them here. In this context, government tourism and transport policies should be as one."

Brosnan's other achievements are equally noteworthy. As chairperson of the Irish Horse Board, he has witnessed the major transition undergone by the horse industry in Ireland over the last ten years when many of the privately-owned stud farms have been sold to international buyers. "Ireland is a good place to breed horses and this has inevitably helped the industry. Irish workers have an affinity with horses and similarly the tax breaks have meant that some of the best stallions in the world are still based here. The industry has not only survived; it has blossomed."

The industry exports £70 million worth of thorough-breds each year and it employs 12,000 people. But the numbers going to race meetings have remained static. As Brosnan explains, "Younger people are not coming through the turnstiles and leisure money has become more difficult to attract. There is huge competition from other leisure pursuits which was not formerly there."

Therefore, the industry must radically change if it is to flourish. Two central problems retard this change. There is a lack of finance and a resistance to change. "The fact is that if you want to run a race meeting, you run it where the population is likely to be today, not where they were thirty years ago. Venues will have to change and courage, commitment, leadership and finance will all have to be invested in the industry."

Although Brosnan is reluctant to knock any commercial success, begrudgery is something he has clear and unambiguous views on. "I hold very strong opinions on the subject. It is a fact that in Ireland if you climb a few steps up the ladder there are people who want to pull you down. I think it is part of the culture and I think it is as strong as it ever was. It is something which probably never will change. It is just part of who we are."

He has found that begrudgery pervades Irish society, he also believes we must sufficiently mature so that it no longer fazes us. "I don't think it should really affect people and it is a matter of getting on with things and what you are trying to achieve," he concluded, before returning to the very many things he and his company, "get on with."

CHAPTER SIX

Help Available

In this chapter, we interview Forbairt's CEO, Dan Flinter, who is chief executive designate of the new State agency, Enterprise Ireland. We also talk to the former Enterprise Minister, Richard Bruton, to see what they, who are at the heart of policy-making, think of what our entrepreneurs have said. We then interview Eoghan Hynes of ISME to get the views of small business. Finally, we interview members of the Irish financial community to see where they believe that banking and finance fit into a successful Irish corporate model.

FORBAIRT

Dan Flinter, Forbairt's chief executive, sees the agency's central tasks as assisting Irish firms to maintain their current growth rates of six per cent by increasing sales and increasing profitability. Although, for strategic purposes, Forbairt helps all Irish businesses, whether they be start-ups, rapid growth firms or self-sustaining companies, Forbairt prefers to lend greater support to those firms deemed to hold rapid growth potential. A considerable amount of Forbairt's resources go to getting these rapid growth firms – with sales of around £500,000 – to target profitable products and services and to improve their management and communication structures.

"The problem is that as you try to encourage these firms, you realise our grave national shortage of key personnel in logistics, distribution and research and development. Even our most promising companies all too often run the risk of failing because they have to export too early in their life cycle. We need to recognise this reality. We might try to use it as part of an analysis about why the world is the way it is, but we just have to accept it as a reality that we cannot change."

Flinter says that the correct marketing decision is dependent upon the sector in question. He cites the Irish software industry as an example where exploiting market niche is the sole viable marketing option open to us. "Irish companies have done extremely well in exporting software, but because of the nature of that industry, it is almost impossible for any country, other than the US, to do well, unless they exploit niche markets."

Echoing Greencore's David Dilger, he emphasises the importance of gaining a strong domestic market presence before trying to crack foreign markets. "Take a company like Martin Naughton's Glen Dimplex. When they started off, many people would never have dreamt they could achieve what they have internationally. You would have expected that they would have to fail in the electrical goods sector, where international brands predominate. They would have proved you wrong. They have done very well and they now hold several international brands." Flinter is well aware that many of our more ambitious firms often fail to gain adequate access to properly priced finance at crucial stages in their development. He has clear views on how this market shortcoming should be tackled. "There have been some improvements in this whole area in recent years. Banks are there to lend money. They behave logically and they have recognised that small business requires a different approach. We must look afresh at our capital markets. To what extent do our capital markets advance the needs of the economy? It's truly time that we began to debate that issue, not from its component parts, but to instead ask that if we were starting off, how would we now design our capital markets."

Flinter believes that State agencies like Forbairt have, by definition, limited capabilities. He believes that a more synergetic approach offers us the best potential for resolving our market shortcomings. To highlight his point, that our larger investment institutions often offer us a sub-optimal service, he comments that "there are companies down the country which have done extremely well, and have been sold to international corporations and I would say that many people in financial institutions in Dublin didn't even know they existed."

Flinter cites the Forbairt innovation of introducing a Developing Companies Market for the stock exchange. When Flinter first mooted the idea with owners of developing businesses "their immediate reaction was positive towards the idea and that is more of the type of contact we need to have". The Developing Companies Market is now up and running with a number of fast growth Irish companies listed on the exchange.

Because entrepreneurs are engaged in creating added value, Flinter believes that they must be allowed to realise some of that added value themselves at an earlier stage in the cycle of their business. "The typical entrepreneur is not a permanent gambler, willing to always risk everything on the next major phase of development. It is important that they be allowed to realise some gain at an earlier point and still be able to bring the business forward."

Flinter believes that we must encourage the few entrepreneurs we do have. "Entrepreneurs, by definition, are a scarce commodity in any society. We in Ireland have very few large companies which have been built up by entrepreneurs and we do have a need for more of them. Our culture must also change so that we recognise entrepreneurial impediments in our national psyche." Flinter does not totally subscribe to the popular view that, historically, we have had a begrudging culture, inimical to fostering an entrepreneurial society. "I don't think we are prisoners of a negative cultural heritage. I don't accept that. There are countless examples since independence where people have funded someone in their area who was starting up a business."

To back up his argument, he cites several well known examples, including that of Royal Tara, where local Galway people put up their own money to start the business. "Our attitudes towards business are changing and this is especially true of people who set up businesses after 1970. But we have come out of a society where attachments of land, security and tenure run very deep in our collective psyche."

Although Flinter accepts the argument that entrepreneurial ability cannot be taught, he accepts Dr Teeling's thesis that education has a part to play in bringing about the desired cultural changes. "The key role of education in developing enterprise is to expose people to businesses and how they are run, in the hope that it will encourage entrepreneurial activity. You have to expose people to different behavioural characteristics. In terms of enterprise, time spent working in a business is an important part of the educational process." In this regard, he praises institutions such as Dublin City University which incorporates work experience modules into almost all of their courses.

He believes that we often fail to correctly pinpoint our real comparative advantages. He again cites Martin Naughton's Glen Dimplex Group which has world-wide sales in excess of £350m. "The notion that comparative advantages are somehow natural and immutable has now been proven to be wrong. Perceived inherited advantages are often overstated. Irish food conglomerates are succeeding not because of the green, green grass of home, they are doing well because they have put successful, experienced management teams in place. They are winning not because they are Irish but because they are producing products which people want."

Flinter is aware of the hostile take-over threats which successful Irish companies face. Whilst he warns against xenophobic tendencies, he agrees with Denis Brosnan that we should, when practicable, try to retain control here. "This is why I believe we have to develop our capital markets in Ireland. If we don't develop them, Irish companies could lose out because we will have a trade sale. In some cases it may be vital for the future growth of an Irish company that it be bought up. But if we can create a capital market which presents an alternative to foreign take-overs, we need to concentrate resources on doing just that. We need a situation where large and successful Irish companies can be taken over by larger and more successful Irish companies."

Forbairt, though aware of the capital and other constraints which our indigenous sector face, wants Irish entrepreneurs to create 12,000 extra jobs net over a five year period. However, to achieve this increase in jobs and to replace the many others which will be lost by natural attrition, the indigenous sector will have to create 36,000 extra jobs by the end of the century. To rephrase that last statement, national sales would have to increase by a massive fifty per cent, from £10.8 billion to £15 billion from 1995 to 2000; annual exports would have to almost double, from £5.7 billion to £9 billion during the same period. Long term, it will be important to see what percentage of this growth is attributable to Irish firms. Clearly, unless something very basic changes in the foreign to indigenous jobs equation, the local, indigenous sector will not, as Dr Teeling has so eloquently pointed out elsewhere in this book, be able to take up the required slack.

And, although the figures do, on the surface, make the IDA's performance look much better than its poorer cousin, Dan Flinter, as Forbairt's chief executive, doesn't begrudge IDA Ireland its recent run of success, where new jobs have so often been counted by the thousand. Flinter points out that the more foreign businesses that are set up in Ireland, the more opportunities there are for indigenous Irish businesses to become suppliers to them. If grant aid is the tool used by the IDA to lure foreign industry to Ireland, then partnership is one of the main tools for indigenous industry to piggy back on the IDA's success.

Forbairt have long-term goals to meet which are inimical to the IDA's rather optimistic, short-term ones. If Forbairt's mandate is to encourage enterprise and to stimulate small business, then it has no business looking for impressive IDA-type job creation results every year – simply because the promotion of entrepreneurship is a slow and pain staking affair which does not lend itself to such instantly quantifiable certainties. This fact is all the more relevant when we consider the small base that Forbairt is trying to build on. Forbairt's clients are, in the main, much smaller than Avonmore, Kerry, Cadbury's, Guinness and the other giants of industrial Ireland. When the average Forbairt client increases its staff by ten per cent, it works out at exactly six jobs – not exactly headline grabbing stuff.

Flinter recognises our many industrial shortcomings and that Irish industry is a delicate plant, needing the support of strategic alliances. Forbairt has signed an agreement with the US Small Business Administration under which each agency will help the other identify suitable partners for their clients. Irish entrepreneurs, in concerns ranging from food companies to the niche computer software sector, have approached Forbairt seeking joint-venture partners, technology transfer deals or simply access to the US market. Flinter believes the scheme is yielding the same kind of concrete partnerships which the North American Partnership Programme, launched in April 1997 with £300,000 in financial support from the International Fund for Ireland, has given.

He is unlikely to be disappointed. The twinning programme has already yielded concrete results for small companies in the border regions. For example, International Test Technologies of Falcarragh, County Donegal, which tests and debugs microprocessors, used the scheme to get an introduction to Cabletron Systems of the US. In Boston, ITT signed an agreement with Cabletron to sell and install its test equipment at Cabletron's US headquarters. It is also part of Forbairt's remit to cut down on our high number of business failures. Forbairt has many low-profile programmes in train to make our smaller companies and entrepreneurs survive and grow. Mentors, auditors, equity backers, technology transfer schemes, partnership programmes, management development programmes are all available.

Forbairt has also concluded that the days of the lone entrepreneur getting an idea and turning it into a self-financing business are now all but over. The day of the team approach has arrived! Experienced and educated managers, for example, are more likely to succeed than inexperienced and uneducated individuals. Forbairt therefore now prefers joint approaches where complementary skills and teams are brought to bear because, in today's more sophisticated world, these types of projects are more likely to succeed than lone, isolated entrepreneurs trying to do everything on their own.

Import penetration has recently increased to just under fifty per cent of total Irish market share. In consumer markets exposed to competition from imports, sales by Irish companies account for less than half of the market. The existing National Linkage programme, which Forbairt run, has so far created some £370 million of additional business in electronics, food, consumer products and technology.

Dan Flinter is particularly proud of the successes Forbairt's mentor programme has enjoyed. More than 1,700 small companies have benefited from this scheme since Forbairt first established it ten years ago – and the number of companies requesting mentor assistance is increasing each year. The Mentor Programme was developed to provide small start-up entrepreneurs with friendly assistance and advice from experienced business people. Flinter says that almost seventy per cent of the participating businesses report that their mentors have helped them to increase sales, profits or employment. Forbairt have a panel of 370 mentors, who are usually relatively experienced and respected in their chosen fields. Until recently, because Forbairt's own target-market was confined to the manufacturing sector, the Mentor Programme was not available to service companies. Now, following the provision of sponsorship from the county enterprise boards and the AIB, service firms can also apply for and be allocated a mentor.

Flinter concludes by arguing: "A team effort is needed. The packages are there from the banks, from ourselves and from other interested parties. Anyone with a good idea and the necessary motivation to succeed should contact us and the other support services. They won't be disappointed."

FORMER MINISTER SPEAKS

Although the former Minister for Enterprise and Employment, Richard Bruton, is aware of Forbairt's path-breaking role, he first of all acknowledged our historical shortcomings when he spoke to us. "We didn't invest in things like research and development and management – the challenge now is to address these weaknesses. Part of that process is to reward the risk takers. Undoubtedly, people in the past tended to put too much store in secure jobs and it is only now we are acknowledging, if people go out, take business risks, make money as a result and then enjoy the fruit of their labour, that that it is a good thing."

The greatest single challenge for small businesses is, Bruton believes, to re-focus themselves to seize today's opportunities. "Manufacturing and assembly are declining in importance and the growth areas are going to be in product design, in innovation, in customer service, marketing and sales, and they are the areas where companies must develop strength and sadly, if you look at the indigenous sector, they are not the areas where we do have natural strengths."

Bruton, in acknowledging the complaints which the small business community level against our banks, agrees with them that Irish banks have been over-cautious in the past. "It is also true that small business has not had a fair shake out. But banks are now providing small business packages and they are moving away from the high collateral approach. I believe we are now seeing the necessary changes in banking policies." Bruton is also critical of the mismatch of funds between lenders and borrowers. "It is quite clear that even though we've seen the emergence in recent years of Irish venture capital funds, those funds have not gone to small or seed start-ups. Indeed the figures would suggest that only £1 in every £20 of venture money is actually going to small start-up companies and that leaves a huge market to be filled."

Bruton wonders why venture capitalists are not going after this market gap more aggressively, although there are signs that venture capitalists are ready to get whatever exposure they can to the booming domestic economy.

Although he accepts that we need a major overhaul of our tax structure, Bruton maintains that this must necessarily be a slow process. "We have come from a situation of having forty per cent corporation tax for indigenous services companies compared to a ten per cent rate for foreign manufacturing firms. One of the effects of this has been that our wealth holders have tended to invest in low risk, rent-giving areas such as property rather than in the socially more beneficial high risk areas such as supporting new start-ups with seed and venture capital. That is what we have come from. But we have to reform our entire set of tax policies to create the necessary environment to achieve our goals. We have to make it cheaper to create employment and I think we moved a good deal in that direction in the 1995 budget."

Bruton does not believe, as the man who oversaw the sale of Irish Steel, that such experiences should warrant a major State sell-off. "Ownership is not the issue. It's about empowering companies to be competitive. We believe in having strong companies in the public sector, but Irish Steel did not have the depth and position to have a viable financial future as it was."

He cites Telecom Eireann as another example of a State-owned enterprise which required a strong partner to bring the company forward and to maintain profitability. He sees the solution in developing the human resource base of the workers in these concerns. Bruton further cites the Telecom example as evidence of the central role education must play in maintaining and developing our competitive advantages in the years ahead. "Currently our system focuses too much on just absorbing material. It needs to be more project-based and practical. This is important in facilitating potential entrepreneurs. Education needs to be geared towards the workplace in terms of the skills that are developed. All of these elements are crucial for Irish competitiveness in the future single European market."

The old IDA was split into IDA Ireland, Forbairt and Forfas. Bruton believes the splitting-up of the old IDA into separate divisions has worked and it has helped us to redress certain structural weaknesses. "Forbairt has bedded down at this stage. But it must be remembered that it is dealing with a sector which has annual profitability rates of around four per cent. The splitting of IDA Ireland from Forbairt had to add value to the whole process, and already it has highlighted the problems we have on the indigenous enterprise front."

He points to Forbairt's innovative programmes, such as its Venture capital fund and its linkage programmes with American companies. Bruton believes that they can do even more. "The agency needs to identify how it can be more dynamic in the services it offers. Clearly, Forbairt has a more difficult agenda than does the IDA, but I believe it is taking a hard look at itself and what it can do."

Bruton points to the considerable growth we have seen in the indigenous software industry, as well as in areas like telemarketing and financial services. He points to our huge potential for growth in services. He targets health and education services in particular. "We need to look at the tradeable services sector. Given that eighty-five per cent of new jobs will come from the services sector over the next few years, we will have to be more independent in this sector and have small companies covering the whole spectrum of the services industry. Clearly, Forbairt have a central role to play in all of this."

SMALL BUSINESS SPEAKS

We earlier discussed our major industrial and service sectors and most of our case studies dealt with major players in those various sectors. We now consider the contribution small business is making to re-orienting our business culture as well as the obstacles which places constraints on its contribution.

Today's small and medium enterprises (SMEs) are faced with opportunities and difficulties specific to our own time. Small manufacturing firms are faced with the reality that the new opportunities offered by the decline in importance of economies of scale are, more often than not, offset by the stringent cost requirements of developing competitive new products and, elements of the high tech sector apart, the difficulty of marketing a wide range of products on a customised basis.

Small can be beautiful and acorns have turned into giant concerns elsewhere. Medium sized firms form the backbone of industrial Germany and similar countries. Nestlé and Rothman, for example, grew from the small towns of Vevey and Stellenbosch, respectively the sizes of Athlone and Maynooth, to strut the international stages in their respective industries.

Why has this not happened in Ireland? There are, of course, the usual suspects: a colonial past, an authoritarian social fabric, a lack of finance – in short, the usual litany of political, structural and other excuses we use to explain away our failures in this area. The reality is not that simple. Our small firms are normally managed by over-worked, hands-on owners with tiny market share and substantial overdrafts. These small business people see much of our current legislation as intrusive, needlessly upsetting the bonds between management and locally hired labour. Their thin profit margins and delicate cash flows make them vulnerable to excessive labour demands. They appear voiceless against our more entrenched interest groups.

The immediacy of their problems delimit their potential for long-term concerted action. Crucially, although Irish start-ups and other measures of Irish entrepreneurship are roughly in line with European averages, Irish failure rates are much higher. Some fifty-six per cent of grant-aided businesses set up in 1983 had gone out of existence ten years later. Ireland is also below average in the number of crucial 'fast growth' businesses it creates. These companies, which have made the greatest contribution to job growth in other countries, have had an almost negligible impact on job creation in Ireland. The high failure rate of SMEs which try to grow is a major source of concern. Over half of the firms assisted under the IDA's Enterprise Development Programme (EDP) from 1978 to 1992 have ceased trading. These were firms identified by the IDA as having the potential to create substantial employment. EDP start-ups in rural areas, Monaghan excepted, had the highest fatality rates.

Reasons for these high failure rates include the problems involved with raising money, rewarding risk and reducing compliance burdens. There is also the need to ensure that small business becomes and remains central to national policy making. These are now each discussed in turn.

Limited financial resources are a fact of life for many small businesses. Although funding does not guarantee success, little can be done without it. The low profitability of Irish companies – around four per cent on sales, compared with around twenty-four per cent for overseas companies operating here – stymies on-going internal funding for both small and large firms. Irish small businesses, in fact, rely inordinately on internal sources of funding. Our new enterprises rely heavily on personal savings for capital; existing enterprises use retained profits as a key source of finance. The availability of start-up funding is therefore critically constrained by our high rates of personal taxation which inhibit saving.

Closely held companies, where five or fewer people control over half the shares, are liable to a surcharge of twenty per cent on their undistributed after tax income. This makes it difficult for such companies to build-up adequate working capital from profits. Further, though there is no indication of an overall shortage of finance in Ireland, our penal tax system dictates that available funds tend to be channelled towards a limited range of relatively low-risk projects.

Small business organisations are all too aware of the problems their members face in the critical area of fundraising. Eoghan Hynes, ISME's founding chairperson, believes that our penal tax rates and the difficulty of securing long-term development and working capital hinders ISME's affiliated members contributing more effectively to job creation.

Hynes is especially critical of the banks. He believes their rates are too high, that their terms for guaranteeing loan approvals to small businesses are too strict and that the centralisation and automation of the decision-making process has reduced the requirements of bank branches to understand their SME customer base. He believes that we have all have lost as a consequence.

"The 1993 Finance Act addressed the problem of seed capital by refunding tax previously paid by the promoters of new enterprises. This scheme, though excellent in principle, has had few take-ups due to a number of factors, many of which centre around its unduly complex structure. Small business needs more long-term finance than the short-term ones which dominate today's market. Special small business loan funds have redressed this historical imbalance somewhat. Although these schemes have enjoyed some success, they still need significant improvements."

"Further, although many of the commercial banks have recently introduced enterprise funds, the premium that Irish small businesses pay on their borrowings – the differential between the prime and AA or small business rate – is now at a record level and among the highest in Europe. This premium may remain high for many small businesses as banks eliminate cross-subsidisation."

Hynes believes that our banks must address a widespread perception that branch managers lack an understanding of business needs and that their lending criteria are too strict. He believes that strategically placed specialised development, business-oriented units might go some way to bridging the wide divide between the banking sector and his members and, following similar reasoning, that the banks should also adopt a code of practice for their dealings with small business customers, along the lines recently introduced in Britain.

The small firm poses a range of acute problems for investment firms and investment subsidiaries of the commercial banks. Their small status and unpredictability involve high administrative costs which the firms begrudge paying; the quality of their management information is usually inadequate due to the dearth of expertise which is endemic to all small firms; because their limited resource base is easily and quickly depleted, they are inherently riskier to fund; because they lack a corporate structure, their success or failure too often depends on the performance of one overworked individual, the actual entrepreneur who owns the concern. All of these factors increase their risk profile in all eyes, except their own.

He acknowledges that our banks are trying to respond. He notes, for example, their Access to Finance Scheme – £208 million at 6.5 per cent fixed for seven years. "The problem is that for the second loan scheme they reduced the time-frame from ten years to seven years. There was no intelligible reason for them to do this. But then again all of the terms of these schemes were drawn up by civil servants and by bankers. Small business was not asked to contribute to the formation of those loan schemes and nobody asked us what we needed."

Hynes is also highly critical of our tax system. He points out that owning a small business requires a major personal commitment and that his members work over fifty-five hours a week on average, putting at risk their personal resources, including their family home. "The chance of failure is not only high but very real and all too common in Ireland for comfort. Yet the returns are low and are reduced further by our tax system. The risk reward trade-off must be improved by reforming taxation and payment practices. Although such tax reforms would bring a cost in the form of lost revenue to the Exchequer, the long-term stimulation which this would give the economy justifies these imputed costs; the reverse stagnation. Our members feel extremely aggrieved by the fact that they are treated less favourably than other tax payers." Hynes suggests some ways that our tax code might be reformed. "A way of rewarding risk that would reflect the national priority of job creation would be to give personal tax credits to business owners who create jobs. The current subsidies are designed solely to play around with the unemployment figures. The low skill levels of the long-term unemployed simply are not marketable."

"Many countries have a lower rate of corporate tax for small companies as a way of encouraging small business and compensating it for the comparative disadvantages it faces. Reform here would have a very positive effect on small firms in the services sector which have accounted for the bulk of additional employment in recent years. It would give these firms extra resources to finance expansion."

He laments our policy-makers' ignorance of our services industry. "A lot of the down-sizing we are seeing from large manufacturing companies is directly impacting on the services sector. So, for example, if a manufacturing company sheds a hundred jobs and then contracts a services company to do the task of that hundred people, while it is increasing the number of jobs in services companies, it is not increasing the total number of jobs created."

Manufacturing and processing should always have a pre-eminent role in policy formulation and that, while tourism may appear to be an exception to this, he argues that tourism jobs will always be low-paid. "If we concentrate too much on those things we will end up with a badly paid, disgruntled workforce."

Hynes bemoans the fact that we lack fiscal incentives to encourage SMEs to retain their earnings. "Our traditionally high corporate tax levels have discouraged our services companies from re-investing their retained earnings. This means the owners tend to live better lifestyles and spend more. If a sliding-scale tax break could be given to them which would be based on re-investing more of their retained earnings into the business, I think it would be useful."

Payment of VAT can aggravate the cash flow problems of small business if they have to remit the tax before they themselves have been paid. VAT, he believes, should instead be payable a cash receipts basis. The present once-yearly payment arrangement of tax for the self-employed causes many difficulties to small, self-employed business tax payers. Hynes also points out that, because the multi-nationals and large, Irish-owned exporting firms are exempt from VAT, the VAT burden is disproportionately shouldered by the SME sector. "The problem is compounded by our VAT collection procedures which, in theory, should not cause cash-based companies a problem. However, the vast majority of manufacturing companies and traded services, dealing in credit, must make good the VAT before they get paid and, therefore, the VAT becomes an up front liability."

Getting paid on time is a never-ending problem for most small enterprises. It causes serious cash flow problems, requires firms to borrow more at disadvantageous rates and consumes an inordinate proportion of scarce management time. While multi-nationals operating in Ireland have a good payment record, the record of Irish firms is often abysmal. Small firms are themselves often amongst the worst offenders; because they are more likely to be paid late, they tend to pay their own creditors late. This becomes particularly objectionable when the company's debtor is the State itself, represented by local authorities, commercial semi-State companies or the Health Boards, where payment delays can be from six to nine months.

Our public sector, the health sector in particular, has had a woeful payment record. This has been improved in recent years with a number of initiatives, but the importance of prompt payment should not be underestimated. Public procurement, purchases by the public sector, accounts for about twelve per cent of GDP and totals over £3 billion annually: many small businesses in the past providing these services have gone out of business as a result of cash flow problems ensuing from being paid late by the Health Boards.

Compliance costs are the quantities of time, money and effort expended by business in fulfilling the administrative requirements placed on them by the State. It is now well-established that these costs are regressive or, in other words, that they bear most heavily on small businesses. Compliance costs are up to 400 per cent higher for smaller firms than for bigger ones. VAT is even more regressive than PAYE. This is mainly because there are economies of scale in compliance, particularly where returns can be computerised. For many small businesses, reducing this paperwork is the single most important thing the State could do to help them.

The owner manager of a typical small manufacturing business is assessed on and must comply with over 1240 (one thousand, two hundred and forty!) issues in the area of PAYE, PRSI, VAT, corporation tax, industrial relations, social insurance, equity legislation, social welfare, central bank exchange controls and stamp duties. This is before other important legislation such as the Companies Act is included. This is a ridiculous burden to place on any business, big or small.

Much of this legislation is rigidly inflexible. Hynes maintains that it is impossible for small firms to adopt in full the kind of Directives coming out of Europe. "The sheer silliness of some of these Directives from a small business point of view is there to be seen by anyone who has some degree of intelligence. The amount of legislation is unbelievable. We have all bent the law in trying to get our businesses up and running. We have all tried to dupe the planning permission laws, we have all lied to our banks about targets and finances. But that is the only way to get things done in this country."

He contrasts our case with the US, where legislation affecting small business is proofed by the Small Business Bureau at the drafting stage.

"In Ireland, the implications for small business are often only looked at after legislation has been passed. This is a ridiculous situation. What then happens is we have to go to politicians and try to get them to see the implications of what has been passed, after it has become legislation. We had some success in this with the Competition Bill. But we could find more productive things to be doing than conduct the political lobbying that this type of nonsense forces us into."

ISME dislikes the fact that business people have no say in the decision-making process which is, they believe, largely run by faceless civil servants largely devoid of any direct business experience. Hynes is calling for co-equal status with big business when decisions about the level of government taxation and spending are being discussed. Hynes points out that membership of a similar body to ISME is mandatory in Germany, Belgium and Holland, while in Turkey its equivalent has two million members and "ministers don't dare move a finger without consulting them first". Although ISME has made repeated attempts to be given equal status with the social partners, they have not, to date, been entirely successful. "The fact is that years ago everyone believed that corporations were going to get bigger and bigger and they would be all that was left. Bureaucrats expected to be dealing with large corporations and they never expected to have to sit down with people who had got their hands dirty by setting-up businesses."

Many of the people sitting on these committees which decide whether a person should get assistance for a business are not equipped to make these decisions. "The agencies are not equipped to make the relevant grant-giving decisions because they are getting input from big business, bankers and civil servants, who know nothing about small business cash flows and little enough about anything else that happens in the business world."

Although he believes that we must, as a matter of urgency, develop an entrepreneurial culture, Hynes realises the enormity of the obstacles impeding progress to that goal. "The best jobs in this country are in the public service. They are risk-free. In that respect we have two very distinct cultures in Ireland, the over-protected, over-subsidised and under-worked public sector and the over-taxed and over-worked private sector."

Inherent to an entrepreneurial culture is the ability to see an opportunity and take risks. Hynes maintains that Ireland is very far from achieving an entrepreneurial culture. "We are all only one generation from the land. Therefore we are not really used to dealing with entrepreneurs and we only have a few of them. We do have a lot of people who take one risk in their lives. They will mortgage their house, or leave a job and take one risk to set up a business. But once it has reached a certain size, they will not take another risk again in their lives. They are not actual entrepreneurs in the real sense of the word."

Hynes loathes our tax system. "It was drawn up before there was a Republic or a Constitution. The modern Irish civil servant is today's equivalent of the rack-renting tax collectors the Normans foisted on us. There is a widespread feeling in the civil service that they actually own the wealth of the country and maybe through tax incentives some of it will be shared out to the mere peasants like our members who create that wealth. They cannot see that the wealth they so arrogantly squander is created by our entrepreneurs operating in the private sector." He sees these fundamental cultural misperceptions as being central to any debate on developing an entrepreneurial culture here. He believes that unless our cultural perspectives change, real progress will not be forthcoming.

Although he is aware of the problems, he is not entirely pessimistic about the future. Eoghan Hynes concludes by musing, "It is in our nature, I think, to be optimistic. There are people coming forward in business even in the current circumstances. If you change the environment, more will come through. We in our organisation want that to happen, because we will all be better off as a result of it."

BANKROLLING BUSINESS

> A feast is made for laughter, and wine maketh merry; but money answereth all things.
>
> Ecclesiastes X.19.

Even though he acknowledges that our banks may have not always adequately responded to the special needs of small and developing businesses in the past, David Ryan – head of small business banking at AIB (1994-1996) – believes that they have become much more proactive in meeting the needs of the sector in the last few years.

Acknowledging that the Irish small business community has, in the past, been over-dependent on short-term debt, he points out that, because more long-term capital is currently available, AIB now find it easier to issue significantly greater amounts of long-term loans, with pay back periods of over twenty years, than they did previously.

Ryan explains that the subsidised loan schemes have been particularly beneficial in this respect. "The second loan fund, which provided funds at 6.5 per cent to eligible companies for terms of up to seven years, was, in fact, subsidised by the banking industry to the tune of fifty per cent. There just isn't a problem with availability of funds in general. Because we cannot respond positively to everyone all of the time, you will always get people who are going to be disappointed with banks. That said, our research shows that seventy per cent of companies seeking increased working capital from banks in Ireland are successful in getting it."

Ryan acknowledges that, in the past, the banking industry tended to insist on undue levels of collateral to secure the loans they issued. "We took the private house out of the equation: we no longer insist on it as collateral; we are, after all, banks, not second-hand house auctioneers. Although personal guarantees must continue to play a major role in the loan applications process, we would prefer a situation where that would not be so necessary." Ryan is, in fact, personally and professionally pleased that the family home no longer features so much in securing business loans. "The question of using the family house in this way was not in the banks' interest; nor was it in the borrowers' interest."

Although more small and growing indigenous companies are now coming forward for loans, Ryan is particularly pleased with the increased numbers of fast growth firms approaching AIB. "Companies in this sector have made considerable progress over the last few years. They are beginning to reach higher levels of profitability. But Irish profit levels are still too low and this will have to improve more quickly in the future."

While he acknowledges that fast growth firms have a vital role to play in our future national well-being, Ryan is adamant that start-ups, if properly nurtured, hold the key to our future. "These companies, if properly managed and financed, can, over time, help us to achieve our national targets. However, we need to address related issues, such as our high tax rates and the cost of employing people here. It is unhelpful that it costs substantially more for employers to increase take home pay for their employees than it does in Britain, for example. Everybody, government official, business person, banker, trade unionist is aware of this malaise. We must tackle it."

Ryan says that, in line with the Culliton Report, all of our major banks are now lending more to firms in our services sector. He has found the take-up of funding from the services sector to be substantial. However, Ryan is quick to point out that AIB does not differentiate between one sector and another when it comes to making decisions on loans. "We are out there to do business. If there is a piece of viable banking business to be done, then we want to do it, because that is why AIB is here. But we want to run with good projects, and there are good projects in all sectors."

"The debt profile of Irish business borrowings is of concern. Almost all of our business loans are for a duration of three years or less; almost fifty per cent for a year or less. This overwhelming dominance of short-term credit is not optimal. We would prefer to more match long-term assets with long-term liabilities and, in this respect, a shift to longer-term credit would provide companies with a better base from which to plan their development."

Ryan cannot understand why, given the constraints of doing business here, Irish banks are regarded as being particularly risk-averse. "The level of loan loss in the late 1980s and early 1990s would not indicate that Irish banks have been less risk averse than their foreign competitors."

He points out that most other European countries have some kind of State guarantee system for small business and that the lack of State support here must obviously change the risk-reward profile of our small companies. Ryan, in rejecting the notion that AIB and Bank of Ireland operate a cosy cartel opposed to the introduction of the third banking force, points out that more than half of AIB's earnings are derived from outside Ireland, and that its Irish-based business must be seen in this light. "I wonder how much more competition would be introduced from a third banking force, when through the amalgamations it would require, we would see fewer players in the market. There are thirty-six lending banks operating in Ireland. Some two thirds of those are foreign-owned. To keep a significant Irish-owned presence in the domestic market, we need to have strong indigenous banks, which can retain sufficient critical mass to survive in the global market."

He believes there is almost always sufficient access to equity for the right projects. "We would have contact with some of the smaller equity institutions and they would often approach us looking for suitable projects to invest in."

Ryan believes that our grant-dependency culture must change. "We need to be able to stand on our own two feet. But that can be difficult in a commercial environment which demeans enterprise. We need to seriously tackle the public finances and taxation in order to address these problems." He maintains that a more efficient tax system is needed to capitalise on any financial reforms that might eventuate. "In terms of capital, if you take venture capital, there is some supply available. There is definitely a short supply of start-up capital and we need to get more people and more institutions to invest in it." This is a priority business issue for AIB Bank.

Although he believes our attitudes to entrepreneurship have matured considerably, he believes that old attitudes persist towards profit making and profit taking. "Our whole attitude to self-employment is changing and that is leading more people to want to set up new businesses. But this change has not been reflected in our attitudes to profit, where we still have this attitude that profit makers are morally flawed. There remains the view that profit is solely there to improve the personal welfare of the individual who made it, as opposed to seeing it as something which can be re-invested in a business to create something of value. This view is essentially self-damaging and needs to change."

Echoing Geoff Read, Denis O'Brien and Eoghan Hynes, Ryan believes that most of our business people are not truly entrepreneurial. "Although increasing numbers of people will take one major risk in their lives in order to set up a business and work for themselves, we still have very few real entrepreneurs who will continue to take risks and go on to create something of considerable value. From that point of view you could say that we are getting very few real entrepreneurs coming through at this stage. I think it will take another generation for that to really change, but I'm sure it will change."

Ryan explains that, when assessing loan applications, AIB looks at the product idea itself, what its market is, what kind of competition there is for the product or service and, finally the individual or team of individuals looking for the loan. "We will look at the people involved and their personal commitment. Ultimately, we make our lending decision on the basis of the people involved in the project."

John Kelly, head of AIB's enterprise development department, deals directly with small business and those interested in start-ups. He says that it is first of all important to understand the motivation of the people applying to AIB for business loans. "When you look at who approaches us for loans, you will often find that they have put some money together, possibly from a redundancy package, and they are interested in working for themselves. We have to assess their track record and use that as a benchmark to gauge their future performances. It's not as easy as some of our critics might like to think. We must be objective, neither too hot and certainly not too cold."

Kelly reckons that the fault is on the demand side, not on the supply side. "If there are shortages, it is not money its good ideas and bankable projects. Very often, our customers want to take on the world. They are too interested in areas where they will have to take on branded goods, and that is extremely difficult. Similarly a lot of the ideas we get in are very hard to bank." Typical deficiencies in applications for small-business loans include the fact they tend to be driven by sole traders, they are reluctant to buy in outside expertise, market research tends to be weak and they often assume that the existing players in the market will not respond to their presence."

"A lot of small businesses and start-ups are too bullish in their financial projections, and sometimes their blind and, one could say, blinkered enthusiasms can get in the way of objectivity." While there is a multitude of State supports from which SMEs can benefit, Kelly has found that his clients very often find it difficult to avail of these supports. "Although bureaucracy may have a lot to do with it, in general they do find it difficult to find their way and get the most out of the funds that are available." Kelly is quick to point out that some good schemes, like the seed capital initiative, have stringent and time-consuming compliance requirements which could be easily and beneficially reformed. "The government must get the correct blend of elasticity and flexibility into their system. At the moment, our borrowers feel that the government demands too much unproductive paperwork. They must address that problem."

Kelly finds that start-up firms often lack professionalism. In particular, they are reluctant to spend money on market research. "Very often they just go with a gut feeling or they go on an observation as to whether there would be a market out there for a product or service. We cannot bank gut feelings and hunches. They must research their ideas and strategies more." For Kelly it is indicative of a person's commitment if they have gone to some expense beforehand which would indicate that, whatever happens, they are determined to go ahead with the project. However, as he laments: "Many start-up applicants will not even have gone to the £400 expense of registering their company in the Companies Office."

He believes that many SME owners have too insular an approach and fail to look beyond their county or regional boundaries. "Most local entrepreneurs will not go to Dublin or Cork and try to get customers outside their region. This is a kind of insular view which is quite common and which, ultimately, can, in a competitive market, be self-defeating."

Kelly admits that lending to the software sector can be problematic. "We don't understand the complexities of some of these projects, so we use AIB IT people to help us at the loan appraisal stage. It's something we are still improving on."

Although the services sector is a growing area of importance to AIB, small engineering related firms still play a pivotal role in their portfolio. Kelly maintains we have numerous back street operations making small parts for large, often foreign-owned plants. Because many of these companies have only one customer, they remain, though profitable, virtually invisible to our policy-makers. "Having only a single customer means they do not have to get out there and market and sell their product. But it does lead to a dependence and that leaves some of them quite vulnerable."

For many of these types of firms, their profits become diluted by diverting them into personal assets. Because profits may not be re-invested into the business, they are prevented from expanding, and this also adds to their vulnerability. "This is why a lot of them are poorly capitalised."

Perhaps reflecting the increasing importance of the services sector where personnel predominate in importance over buildings, machinery and other fixed assets, John Kelly again emphasises that people hold centre stage in their lending-criteria analysis. He divides his prospective customers between the dreamers and doers. The dreamers he politely, professionally and perfunctorily dismisses. "Because we too must watch our bottom line – banks, at the end of the day, can only be interested in finished products because, unless the product comes to fruition, the bank loan cannot be repaid. We cannot live with levels of bad debt."

Like Denis Guiney, Kelly agrees that market opportunities are ever present. However, unlike Guiney, Kelly is not an entrepreneur. He is a cautious banker and, as such, he emphasises that the entrepreneurial concept must be explained in its entirety to the bank, who will then determine if, in their view, the identified gap in the market means that there is a market in the gap. Banks must, in other words, cast a cold, professional eye on all proposals brought to them. It is for that reason that they like to see the would be entrepreneur armed with a well presented business plan.

"A well presented business plan brings into greater focus several home truths centred around the entrepreneur's borrowing and business record. Generally speaking, market gaps exist because of down-sizing, outsourcing, exiting by an existing player or because an opportunity to avail of import substitution exists. Unique products or untried services are generally hard to bank as there is no financial form from which the bank can extrapolate into the future. Once-offs cannot constitute a template for banks to evolve their lending policies on."

Tom Barry, a Director of Corporate with AIB, deals with companies seeking to borrow £2 million or more. Typically this type of company makes profits of at least £1 million per year. For established companies with the kind of track record that allows them to make this level of profit, Barry believes there is an oversupply of debt finance available in the Irish market. "In some respects I would love to be an entrepreneur out there looking to borrow to expand my business. If you have a business, which is making profits of £1 million per year, you will get any number of banks to lend you the money you require."

Barry points out that this increased competition in the corporate lending sector has meant that AIB and our other Irish banks have altered the models they use to assess how much established companies can borrow when making acquisitions. "We have refocused the emphasis away from assets and equity, so that established companies can now borrow on multiples of the combined profits of their own business and the company they will be acquiring."

Barry maintains that there is an over-supply of lending banks which has driven down the price of borrowing. "I don't have any clients who are solely dependent on AIB for their banking needs. Therefore, generally speaking, you can take it that, if their proposals are viable, they will be banked at a price that is certainly not excessive for the risk level they present. If AIB mis-price its facilities, our customers will go to our competitors. We are here to lend and, like any other business, we must keep the customer happy and provide the services the customer wants at the best price available. If we do not provide the service the customer wants, someone else will and we will lose that custom. We must, however, charge a commercial price for the risk involved. We cannot give our services away free, gratis. That would not be sound business on our part. We must price our services in accordance with the risk attached to them."

Barry is aware of the image that business lobby groups and similar organisations have of the Irish banking sector. He does not agree with their analysis. "Business associations sometimes claim that we are loathe to lend out money. That is simply not true. A sensible proposition from any profitable established business will be treated favourably. The only thing that stops banks from lending is where the risk is just too high. Management within banks have an incentive to lend. We have new business budgets and targets like any other business. We have an incentive to look favourably on any viable project brought to our attention. That is the nature of a bank. It is like any other business enterprise. However, we have a duty of care to our savers and shareholders to be prudent with the funds entrusted to us."

Barry believes that companies at an earlier stage of development need a greater level of entrepreneurial risk capital. "Sometimes, they seek to rely too heavily on borrowing which is inappropriate for their stage of development. On occasions, banks are criticised for not providing loans for a debt return whereas in reality it is an equity risk."

Unlike loan capital, equity capital does not guarantee the investor a return; it is instead dependent on the performance of the enterprise. In start-up and early stage fast growth businesses where the prospects of success or even survival are uncertain, high levels of debt funding are inappropriate. Equity capital is regarded as being best suited for these projects: it means that the entrepreneur does not have to fund borrowings when cash in-flows are uncertain; it allows the investor to obtain high profits if and when they succeed and to take the risk of loss when they fail. Banks do not have such an equity upside when businesses succeed and hence cannot take the loss when they fail.

There has been a welcome change in the availability of private capital. In the last three years almost £10 million in early stage venture capital has become available through the efforts of Forbairt, the EU and the private sector. Barry believes there are not enough companies of suitable size anxious to press ahead and aggressively seek new foreign markets with the over-abundance of debt funds currently available in the Irish market. "The fact is that the banking sector could service dozens more companies making profits of about £1 million or more. I'm not being critical of Irish business people. Some businesses don't want to think bigger. The domestic market is so small that if they are really going to succeed on a large scale, they need to work on expanding overseas. The number of entrepreneurs, who have reached this size with their business and who want to take the big risks involved, is small."

Similarly, our entrepreneurs are often reluctant to allow others take an equity stake in their enterprises. This attitude also impedes indigenous

Irish companies from floating on the stock exchange. In the past the Irish stock market did show limited appetite for small companies seeking to raise capital. In recent years, particularly with the progress of the Developing Companies Market there has been a welcome change in this with a number of companies, many quite small, coming to the DCM and being well-received and raising capital on very attractive terms.

Barry is optimistic about the future development of large scale indigenous Irish companies. He believes that, despite greater international competition across virtually all sectors, and despite ever-tightening profit margins, we will see more Irish companies growing to be of international ranking in their own right. "Margins are becoming tighter, but Irish entrepreneurs are responding to it by tightening their costs. They are very careful with their entrepreneurial investment. They have specialist teams to identify and manage the investee companies following the acquisition. They continue to expand carefully and consistently over time and therefore they will succeed. And AIB and the other Irish banks will be with them all the way."

Although Forbairt has been involved in this end of the market, their equity role has tended to have special characteristics which set it apart from the growth-oriented investment of venture capital companies. Firstly, a principal objective has been to reduce the cost per job and to ensure a measure of repayability to the State, rather than in filling a financing gap for fast-growing companies. Secondly, equity stakes are held at about ten per cent to avoid issues of control arising. Thirdly, board representation does not normally arise, implying a hands-off approach to management issues. Fourthly, second-round financing is not generally available. Clearly, a more pro-active involvement, within current expenditure guidelines, would encourage our financial sector to invest more heavily in our viable firms.

So could the private sector. A number of fund management companies have, in fact, come forward with investment structures designed to cater specifically for investment by the funds in small and medium-sized companies. However, we need more efficient utilisation of the structure which we already have. Further bureaucratic layers, unless they bring more resources into play, will only worsen an already weak situation.

The perceived shortage of finance for new company formation of the requisite quality reflects the fact that our funds management industry, which controls the bulk of our savings, is focused primarily on investments in large, developed companies and liquid securities, both in Ireland and overseas. The banking system concentrates on shorter-term, secured lending and on less risky investments.

The Irish market is very concentrated. Although there are over eighty firms listed on the Irish market, the top four companies account for over fifty per cent of total market capitalisation. These problems of concentration in the equity market are compounded by a high degree of concentration in the fund management industry. The top three fund managers between them control more than seventy-five per cent of all funds under management. As a result, if fund managers were to devote a high proportion of their funds to the Irish equity industry, they would end up with portfolios with a high degree of stock-specific risk and a very skewed sectoral exposure. Because they therefore diversify by investing overseas, Irish SMEs lose out.

The larger institutional firms prefer to concentrate only on firms with market capitalisations of £100 million or more. In the Irish case that means only the very biggest firms, or in other words, significantly less than one per cent of all Irish firms. So, the vast majority of Irish firms have no effective means by which to gain access to institutional funds.

The Irish stock exchange therefore remains largely irrelevant as a means of raising finance for the vast majority of Irish industrial firms. The Small Companies Market, which was established in the mid-1980s specifically to cater for the needs of growth-oriented smaller firms, has not proved successful, with only four firms currently being listed.

Tom Healy, general manager of the Irish stock exchange, has instituted a Developing Companies Market in Dublin, specifically designed to cater for the needs of those small and medium-sized companies, which are poised for rapid growth. It began with discussions with Forbairt and the Department of Enterprise and Employment on how the new market would play a positive, pro-active role in helping to provide equity capital to cash-starved fast growth companies. The DCM came about for very good reasons. The fact is that when companies are very small or new, there are a number of structures or supports which they can receive. When they get slightly bigger, there are schemes, like BES, which have helped but they have not been as successful as originally intended."

Developing companies have found it difficult to tap into the huge funding resources of the capital markets. There has been an image that the stock exchange was only for big business. The notion has also persisted that it is expensive to float the business and the company has to comply with all of the disclosure requirements on salaries and financial performance. These notions are now being expelled.

Healy and his stock exchange colleagues have devised a set of disclosure and other requirements which are more geared for the needs of our smaller developing companies. The new market is largely modelled on the Alternative Investment Market (AIM) of the London stock exchange, which is geared towards small developing companies.

Although some British companies which are capitalised at just over £1 million have gone for a London listing, companies capitalised at between £5 million and £10 million have been more typical of the successful firms. There are numerous companies of that size in Ireland which could benefit from a listing, where their shares will be traded in the same way as any other quoted company.

Although the financial markets are important, tax considerations tend to play a big role in Irish investment decisions. Geoff Read, Denis O'Brien, Eoghan Hynes and several of the other entrepreneurs we interviewed have already outlined many of the entrepreneurial disincentives in our tax system. There are, of course, many more. However, whatever the desirability of using the tax system to encourage productive investment, the tax system should not discriminate against such investments. At present, the tax system provides direct incentives for a number of low-risk savings options, including pension funds, life assurance funds, freedom from capital gains on gilts, the favoured tax treatment of owner-occupied housing and special savings and investment accounts. These tax incentives for low-risk investments discriminate against direct investments by individuals in more economically productive areas. Of course, this is not the only barrier to productive investment. However, given society's interest in promoting risk investment, it is not desirable to provide tax incentives to channel resources to low-risk areas. The government is realising this now with the moves to curb house prices in Ireland, as a higher percentage of houses bought are for investment.

Company profits are taxed at a higher rate than dividend payments; thus when the company pays shareholders a dividend, the shareholder does not receive the full tax credit as the company tax rate is higher. By not passing on the full tax credit, the government is effectively increasing the amount of tax recovered from both the company and shareholders.

For most small Irish companies, this double taxation leads to an incentive for proprietary directors to withdraw all profits as salary rather than retaining and re-investing profits and taking a dividend at a later stage in the company's development.

Section 115 of the Finance Act 1986 provides that where the Revenue Commissioners are owed outstanding PAYE and VAT by a debtor, they may oblige another creditor of that debtor who is secured by a fixed charge on book debts to pay over all or part of whatever funds had been obtained from the debtor. The effect of section 115 is to confer on the Revenue Commissioners a kind of super-preferential creditor status which is neither desirable nor necessary. For many trading companies, their book debts are the main source of collateral they can offer to banks in negotiating a loan. As a result of section 115, the value of book debts as a security has been considerably diminished.

Banks have indicated that section 115 has had an adverse effect on their willingness to lend to small business and on the terms on which they do so. The operation of this section has also led to a greater than desirable emphasis on fixed asset-backed loans under the Small Business Expansion Loan Scheme.

Although all political parties and interest groups agree that our tax system must be overhauled, we argue in our concluding chapter that, because it is at least as important that anti-business preconceptions and prejudices must also change if we are to take advantage of the many opportunities which continue to come our way, these groupings must tackle these underlying beliefs with the urgency, honesty and decisiveness that they deserve. The halving of Capital Gains Tax in the 1997 budget and the further reductions in tax rates were important steps in the right direction.

Clearly then, the creation of a vibrant and viable entrepreneurial culture in Ireland is a multi-faceted problem needing complex solutions, some of which we now touch on in our final chapter.

CHAPTER SEVEN

What is to be done?

Our introduction made our basic point. It was that our entrepreneurs, those who have the uncanny ability to make us more productive and therefore more prosperous, should be encouraged to be more involved in our nation. Our subsequent chapters, by allowing Irish entrepreneurs to air their views on our economic potential, merely fleshed out our reasons for making that simple statement.

We hope that our book also made some other things apparent. There are, for example, many people, many organisations and many institutions trying, despite our cultural inheritance of begrudgery and related ailments, to make our economy more vibrant. Many of them have, by anyone's yardstick, achieved fantastic results. More importantly, perhaps, they have shown us that we can be successful, even in the most competitive and non-traditional arenas. They have given us a template on which to build a successful economy.

This template is popularly known as the Celtic Tiger. This economic transformation came into being partially as a result of EU structural funds being channelled into the value-added sectors of our economy. Those EU funds will soon dry-up. It will then become all the harder for us to maintain the standards we are becoming used to. Our entrepreneurs will play an increasingly pivotal role in maintaining our economic vibrancy.

Since these interviews were conducted these entrepreneurs have continued to excel. Denis O'Brien has floated Esat Telecom on the Nasdaq; Carol Moffett has sold her company to Powerscreen; Rye Valley is in the process of being sold to a major Irish food processor; Glen Dimplex, Norbrook, the Kerry Group and Ray Kearns, all remain very active in their chosen fields; Forbairt – who are set to merge with the Trade Board – and the AIB continue their supportive roles to our entrepreneurs, both big and small.

Clearly these are vibrant people and organisations adapting well to the dynamics of the modern marketplace. In recounting their stories, we have tried to capture some of this dynamism and to thereby show how and why our entrepreneurs and experienced business people must be given a pivotal role in navigating our economic future.

Because these people are trying to maintain the Celtic Tiger, the tax and other obstacles debilitating their efforts must be suitably amended. They, as much as those who live on the taxpayers' largesse, must have their say so that a richer, more inclusive Ireland can emerge to overcome the challenges of the future.

Much of what is to be done has been spelt out not only in this book, but in weightier ones such as the Culliton and Moriarty Reports. Many of these reforms and strategies seem obvious enough, as obvious that no great change will occur until we adopt a more progressive, pro-active pragmatic business culture which replaces the navel gazing of the past with a more pro-active, entrepreneurial approach to building the viable Ireland we need to pragmatically meet the challenges of tomorrow.

We must, in other words, give our entrepreneurs their due and encourage them to grow the two blades of grass where only one now grows. We must also play a role and not merely be content to watch the new blades of grass grow. We too must roll up our sleeves and hasten that day.

Index

ALSO AVAILABLE FROM BLACKHALL PUBLISHING

Transforming Leadership

TERRY ANDERSON

"*Transforming Leadership* is a must read for anyone who wants to make a difference in the future. It presents ways we can respond to these uncertain times and help everyone, including ourselves, win."

Ken Blanchard, co-author, *The One Minute Manager.*

This much talked about executive and management self-development book goes beyond the traditional boundaries to define the relationship between leadership performance and corporate performance optimisation. It is aimed at managers who have moved beyond HRD buzzwords and slogans, and provides them with a clear insight into the distinct elements that cultivate leadership to develop high quality and performance.

Through a straightforward, integrated method, the individual self-evaluates his or her leadership qualities and skills, then begins to enhance them by implementing specific learning actions that are backed by powerful coaching and mentoring support.

The book is written in a friendly, personal and above all accessible manner and demonstrates clearly and practically how anyone can improve their leadership skills and cultivate a workplace culture in which effective leadership means effective performance.

Terry Anderson is a results-oriented consultant, executive coach, author and university lecturer.

336 pp. ISBN: 1-901657-39-6 £19.99 pbk September 1998

Competition in the 21st Century

Kirk WM Tyson

Business competition will change radically in the next century. Short-sighted companies will go out of business. Survivors will successfully make the transition from the so-called Information Age of this century to the Intelligence Age of the 21st century.

Ten years in the making, this book paints a picture of the competition of the future which is based on in-depth research of world-wide business over the past 100 years. It shows business competition in its 19th Century childhood, 20th Century adolescence, and 21st Century adulthood. The book highlights new beginnings – the Intelligence Age, highly networked "MegaStrategic Entities", and the need for both a "Competitive Knowledge Base" and a "Perpetual Strategy Process" to provide an early warning system for executives.

Tyson provides the key characteristics of successful companies, leaders and business practices of the 21st Century, and covers business in Europe, North America and the Asia/Pacific region. Dozens of companies are profiled, including Nestle, 3M, Toyota, Royal Dutch Shell, Procter and Gamble, Sony – and many more.

Kirk WM Tyson is a business consultant, researcher, author and speaker of world-wide acclaim. He is the chairman of Kirk Tyson International, Chicago, with offices and affiliates throughout Europe, North America and the Asia/Pacific region. He is the author of *Business Intelligence* and *Competitor Intelligence Manual and Guide*.

ISBN 1-901657-33-7 £19.95 pbk June 1998